Living
Broke
SUCKS!

By:

Mark A. Tuschel

© 2015

<u>Dedication:</u>

"This book is dedicated to you the reader.

*Without **you** there wouldn't be much purpose for me to write.*

I thank you."

Mark A. Tuschel

Legal Mumbo Jumbo

Living broke SUCKS!

Published 2015 by: CW Media, Inc.

All inquiries about this book, including interviews, purchases or speaking engagements can be made through email: **booksales@LivingSoberSucks.com**

Please do not bother contacting the Library of Congress Cataloging-in-Publication Data. They have enough problems of their own and they're pretty busy from what I hear.

ISBN 13: 978-0-9898747-9-3

Table of contents

Foreword

By: Jeff Rendall

The author and I met through membership at an athletic club. We both have no fear in talking to strangers and enjoy meeting new people. As we stayed fit and talked, we found out that we had many things in common and had lived through a lot of similar life experiences. Mark is a person dedicated to helping those that want to be helped. Like me, Mark has worked hard, made changes to improve his life, and continued to build skills and gain knowledge. Mark has built a business and written previous books directed at changing and improving one's life. When Mark asked me what I did, I told him I had worked professionally for thirty years, but now manage financial resources accumulated over time.

I have told Mark and others that you can work for money or your money can work for you. Mark and I agree money allows people to transfer value from one another for the essentials needed to survive. In life, money is the only thing!

The key word in the title of this book relates to *not* having enough money to live the way that you would like. Unless born into the legacy of a wealthy family, most of us have been broke at some point in our life. Being broke can be caused by a single event that one can't control, but in most cases its patterned behavior that one grows up with or discovers on their own. I've been broke twice. I was broke when I finished school, and when exiting the military two and a half years later. I was close to broke the entire time in the military, but there were subsistence level paychecks to live on. So when I was broke, it wasn't for a week or a month, it was for a while, and generally there wasn't much fun in my life. Being broke creates a lot of tension, conflict with friends and family members and is outwardly embarrassing. It's tough saying 'I don't have the money' when asked to do something with family or friends.

I knew this was not the way I wanted to live and used my skills to build a career and break the cycle of being short of money to live as I wished. I did some foolish things early in my adult life, but eventually made the right choices and started to build some net worth and was able to eventually live comfortably. Over time I learned new skills in accumulating and managing money and found a way to have the money I had accumulated work for me. This is a long journey that requires focus, continuous learning, and not giving in to specific wants. Essentially you can't spend more than you earn.

You know when you're broke. Nobody walks up and says, "Hey, you're broke." You could be a little bit broke, moderately broke, or desperately broke. The situation goes from just being able to cover expenses on a short term basis, to occasionally borrowing to cover expenses, to exhausting any credit available, to looking like you're going to be homeless or fully dependent on the generosity of others. The symptoms go from, you have no cash, you've borrowed from friends and relatives, you're late or not paying bills for essentials to live, any credit is maxed out, pawnshops become a source of revenue, and a long list of others desperate measures to find money.

There are many reasons one can be broke. First of all, as unfortunate as it may be, you grew up in a family that was broke and it is all you ever knew. You have difficulty maintaining employment that supports you or a family; due to the negative influence of others, substance abuse or other dependencies, inappropriate lifestyle decisions, or your personal skills don't have a lot of value to an employer. Single or related unplanned events can be financially devastating. Serious illness, marriage or divorce, birth of a child, arrest and incarceration, and others can have a huge effect on the revenue or expense side of your life.

To find a way out of the 'broke condition' you have to understand who you are and what you can do to get out of the situation. First of all you have to evaluate your skill set and how to use it in generating the revenue to survive. This includes; reading, writing and speaking skills, mechanical or trade skills, emotional stability, and many others that will get you employed and give you mobility to higher paying positions. Your skill set has to contain knowledge of value to an employer, the ability to work with others, and the capability to deliver value to the market place. As you work your way out of the 'broke situation', you will develop self-worth as you effectively deal with getting un-broke. You will find a new sense of self-confidence, gain knowledge that you will make the right decisions, not react to emotional impulse, and find ways to stretch the value of money available to meet your needs.

For your benefit, you will have to stay focused and do the correct things over and over again. You can't fall back into the same trap that got you broke in the first place. There will be many negative influences. Don't let them side track you. You can't fall victim to the promise of some scheme looking 'too good to be true', because they don't exist. Lotteries and casinos are set up for you to lose. Making excuses and shifting the blame won't work. If you do something stupid, admit it, document it if you have to, and don't repeat it.

You need to take from this book a few good ideas that work for you in the environment you live. What works for you may be completely different than what works for someone else. Build a plan that has specific strategies to keep cash in your account. Some people refer to the word 'budget', but I think 'plan' is a better term, because a plan grows and develops, and a budget is just part of the plan. Both long and short term goals need to be established and prioritized. Key measures are important and must set up and maintained on a periodic basis. Some measures will be daily, weekly, monthly and annually. Documentation is the only thing that will make this a successful project. An accounting degree is not required, but you will need to manage numbers accurately. You need to know where you have been on this journey, identify mistakes or areas for improvement from the data, and project where you want to be in the future. Periodic evaluations and course corrections are a necessity. Define the cause for things you should have done differently and develop and implement a corrective action plan. You want to spend less than you bring in, save and get out of debt, and eventually build net worth.

Pay attention to your money and where it goes and the value it buys every day. Ignore others that tell you what your doing is a waste of time. They probably are or will be deeper in a financial mess than you. Get input from others you trust; search out and use resources that bring value to your plan and life; and keep it simple to start and let it grow as confidence builds. Be your own best advocate; proud of your success; and use your mistakes as learning tools. Take a break and give yourself a reasonable reward that is part of your plan when appropriate.

Enjoy new found freedom that having money to provide the essentials of life and some luxuries for yourself and the people around you. Share your knowledge with others that recognize the changes you have made and if this book made the difference, share it with others or tell them where to find a copy.

Remember – Money is the only thing!

Introduction:

This book isn't a get rich quick system. The purpose of this book is to get you thinking about what money is, what it can do for you, what it can't do for you, how much of it you believe you need, how to use it wisely for your own benefit and how not to become a slave to it. My biggest wish is that you learn ways to be comfortable with the subject of money, how to genuinely enjoy your money and how to get the most utility out of it, no matter how much or how little of it you have.

Too many people are afraid to be honest with themselves about money. They fear that they'll look greedy if they pursue money but at the same time they fear being poor. Some people even fear wealth—believing that wealth is evil or that they aren't deserving of it. The biggest problem that I see in others (and I have been guilty of this myself), is a level of denial and innumeracy. Innumeracy is far different than being financially illiterate. Most adults aren't financially illiterate—they know basic math (2+2=4, 10–6=4, etc.). Innumeracy is when someone does not understand the power of interest, compounding, and hidden costs or they're deluded by percentage numbers. They are innumerate when they want $10 to buy them $20 worth of goods or they "buy now" in anticipation of earning the money tomorrow.

Constantly giving disclaimers is distracting from the message. So let me give you my disclaimers right now. I use possessive and general words such as: you, we, us, our, they, them. These words are not intended to describe or categorize the entire human populace as a whole. These words are used to simplify and speed up the reading process, and to make the book more personal. Other terms like "He" or "She" aren't gender specific. Generalities are not intended to project prejudice so don't let my use of them distract you from the matter of the material. Additionally, I cannot be held responsible for you living better. As you learn ways to get more utility out of your hard-earned money, I hope you become inspired to save, invest and become wealthy, allowing you to live a comfortable existence. I receive no royalty or commission from your wellbeing. You've already (presumably), paid for this book and that's royalty enough for me. I also cannot be held liable for any losses you may incur, financial or otherwise.

Polished psychobabble and an expansive vocabulary are pretty, but there's nothing pretty about being broke. So I'm going to speak in simple, straightforward words. You might disagree with many of my philosophies. And you know what? That's great! Because that means that *YOU* are engaged in reading and thinking on your own behalf. I purposely don't use technical terms or economist jargon. I attempt to give real world examples. The examples I give may not be conditions from your life or things you've done, but I'm confident that they will clearly illustrate my points.

Everyone's behavior, opinion, perception and situation are different. If something in particular doesn't apply to you then please don't take it personally. And while an opinion or behavior may not apply to you, it may apply to someone you have to deal with, who you are friends with or care about.

Even if a behavior doesn't apply to you, it may have applied to you at one time in your life or it may influence your thinking once in a while. I will be the first to admit that I have fallen prey to most (if not all), of these behaviors or assumptions about money at one point or another in my life. I still must be watchful of these unconscious influences. So please do not feel as if I am deriding or lecturing you. If I were to be "politically correct" or try to be delicate about certain subjects the importance and the message would not come across.

Awareness of how much money is *coming in* and how much money is *going out* is the key to getting the most utility out of your money. Everything is an exchange and money is worthless until it is spent or exchanged for something else. Please don't interpret this as me telling you to spend every penny you have. The goal is to enjoy some of your hard-earned money and retain some of it to allow you to be calm knowing that you have a little security.

As you read, I would like you to notice the difference between my book and the thousands of others out on the market regarding money and wealth. First off, I don't tell you how to get rich or whether you should be rich. My goal is to get you thinking about what money means to you and about how you can enjoy and get the most out of what money you have.

Many other financial gurus will say, "Don't spend your money on this, don't buy that, save your money here, etc." How do they know what's enjoyable to you? How do they know what your conditions actually are or what your desires and goals are? I present observations and ideas and YOU need to be involved in your own decisions.

The biggest difference is that I don't believe you have to live a Spartan existence and rob yourself of enjoyment. You'll read a common theme through this book: **"Money is worthless until it is spent, invested or leveraged."** That doesn't mean you burn through every penny you earn or have, it means that your money is "used" in some fashion. It may get "spent" by putting it into a savings account for peace of mind.

I won't be telling you what you should do with your money. It's YOUR money and I don't have to live your life. The principles I share with you work—and do work for me—but you need to do some thinking of your own and take control and ownership of your own financial condition.

The other theme you will read is: "Everything is an exchange." If you really get pleasure from your morning cup of Starbucks coffee, why rob yourself of that joy? But *that* purchase is an exchange. That money is now gone and you will have to forgo something else. Many financial "talking heads" criticize the daily purchase of Starbucks coffee. They will present a mathematical equation showing how much it costs you weekly, monthly, annually and how much you would be worth after 20 years of investing your Starbucks money based on perfect annual returns and compounding. Great, so you scrimp, save and sacrifice for 20 years for what? So you can now afford Starbucks in your waning years, drinking coffee while your false teeth fall in the cup? If Starbucks brings you genuine joy now, then buy it, but remember that you have exchanged a small amount of tomorrow's security for today's joy.

I do give examples for the cost of smoking or drinking. I show you how much money can be amassed by eliminating (or moderating), some of these habits from your life and doing something useful with the money **not spent** on these habits. But I won't be telling you what to do. I'll just be showing you the math. What you do about it is your own choice.

Another theme you'll read is: "Money isn't everything." But at the same time it's the only thing. Without money you can't live. Money can't buy you everything, but it can buy you a lot of things and it can help you feel secure and calmer. Money will not buy you *genuine* friendship or love, but it can buy you fake friends and temporary lovers. People say, "Sex changes everything." Oh no, sex only changes some things, MONEY changes everything. Money changes relationships.

If all you want to do is stay a few dollars ahead of your paycheck, that's fine. That's your choice. If you want to get the most utility out of your money, and pleasantly surprise yourself by amassing a bit of wealth and a security net, I believe this book will help you. But YOU will have to do the work to earn the money that comes in and then control the amount that goes out. No matter what your financial or wealth goals are, and no matter what your current financial condition is, I believe this book will enlighten you and help you better understand money. This book won't *make* you wealthy—YOU must take action and make yourself wealthy. Apply a few of the strategies, concepts and principles and YOU will be able to be proud of yourself because YOU did the work— not me.

We can spend our entire lives searching and waiting. Waiting for the day that everything comes together and everything is perfect—the day that we become wealthy—then we'll be happy. Why wait? Why not start working on your own wealth and happiness now? As a good friend of mine said, "It's never too early to start." Don't wait. Don't be afraid of math or money.

So let's hop right in and begin getting comfortable and familiar with your friend: *Money*.

Chapter #1

What is money?

"Money isn't the root of all evil, people are."

What *is* money? You might think this is a rather dumb question, but through understanding what money actually *is* and its *purpose* you can better understand how to use it.

Money is a tacitly agreed upon means to **barter** for goods or services among buyers and sellers. You barter your time and talents for wages. The pieces of paper (money) which you bartered your time and talent for can now be used by you to barter for things you need or want. Money is also a means for traceable and fixed taxation on those wages, products and services exchanged.

If we didn't have money, each and every transaction would require you to negotiate the value of a transaction. "I'll knit you two pairs of mittens for 5 gallons of gas." The problem is that the person selling the gas to you may not be interested or in need of your mittens. A pair of mittens during January in Minnesota may be worth 20 gallons of gas but they will be worthless in Florida during the month of July. The seller of gas may take your mittens in trade so he can barter your mittens for something else, but that's only if he knows someone else will want the mittens. Or he may just keep the mittens until he finds someone that is interested in mittens. So the person trading you his gas may want six pair of your mittens instead of two and only offer you three gallons of gas in return. All of this product bartering would be a storage nightmare for the gas seller (having to house numerous items bartered for), along with the uncertainty of not knowing if or when someone will want mittens, biscuits or something else.

This would all be too difficult and time consuming for both of you. You may never end up getting the things you need or want through a barter system. So money is an agreed upon, quantifiable means of exchange.

Governments also want in on a piece of the action. Money is a way for exchanges to be taxed. It would be rather difficult for our government (any government) to receive a piece of a barter transaction. For instance, let's say I trade you two pounds of butter for a blanket. The government doesn't want a teaspoon of butter and a small section of the blanket as tax on our transaction; they want a piece of the money. Bartering still exists. I barter my services to help you stain your deck and you help me out by cooking me a steak dinner. People (privately) trade products or services all the time, but when they do, the IRS wants to know what products or services you bartered to establish a mathematical value so they can collect their share of tacitly agreed upon tokens; money.

So we know that money is a recognized and tacitly agreed upon means of making exchanges. Let's consider the purpose of money, which is similar to the definition of what it is, but with a few twists. The purpose of money is so we can exchange it for services and products without having to negotiate a barter value for each and every deal we make. If you have enough "tokens" (money) then you can purchase the product or service you desire. Money can be quantified and readily carried (cash, checks, debit card or credit card). By quantifying it, you then know how much of a good or service your tokens will buy.

A brief history of money.

Who invented money? Well, about 3,000 years ago some old Greek guy named Pocketous Fullofcashus **didn't** just come up with the idea one weekend and start a bank the following Monday morning and begin handing out his new invention called money.

What we now know as "money" evolved over thousands of years. It wasn't planned or even invented, it simply emerged.

People had been bartering their goods for many years, trading figs for pottery. But let's say that I had an overabundance of dried figs and I wanted some pottery but the pottery maker didn't need or want any more figs. You happen to be my neighbor and you do want some figs but all you have to trade me is some raw tin. I would have to trade you my dried figs (before they got drier) for your tin. Then I would have to find someone who had pottery that is interested in acquiring some tin. This is time consuming and I might never find a pottery maker who is interested in tin. This would mean that I'd have to trade my tin (which I acquired by trading my figs) for something else, then something else, until I found the right "goods" the pottery maker was interested in or needed. While all this running around and trading of "goods" was taking place, I also had to concern myself with what food I would eat today (I'm sick of figs), what pestilence or disease will I catch, oh, and here comes the invading Hun army to slaughter everyone and take all my goods that I can't carry when I run.

So if I wanted to trade for things, this would mean that I would need to have large inventories of all kinds of various other goods that I would be able to trade with, depending on what the other person wanted or was in need of. This massive warehousing of goods for each person was impossible.

That's when people figured out—all on their own—that certain items were considered to be valuable to almost everyone and could be traded *in lieu of goods*. If I had some of these "mutually agreed upon valuables" I didn't have to go searching around for actual items or goods to trade. I could trade (sell) you my figs for something of mutually accepted value, gold pebbles for instance. Then I could take the gold pebbles to my local pottery maker and trade a few pebbles for pottery. The pottery maker could then trade the pebbles I traded to him for something he wanted. What we were bartering was a mutually agreed upon valuable. This is an extremely simplified example of the emergence of money.

It wasn't called money at first. Various minerals, jewels and substances viewed as "valuable" were used for exchange. There was no real standard of worth on any of these things, so you and I still had to negotiate and there wasn't much fair trading going on. There was always the risk that the "valuable" we were trading wasn't authentic, the first instance of counterfeiting. Literacy and cognition of mathematical basics wasn't widespread, so one of us was probably going to get ripped off in our transaction.

That's when governments stepped in. (The term government is used to represent Emperors, Kings, Dictators, etc.) Early civilizations and empires used "coins" formed from precious metals that its citizens could use as a means of trade. That gave the government control over how much "money" was floating around in civilians' hands. Then someone (in government of course) figured out that if the government held on to the precious minerals, jewels or substances and then stamped their own official coins made from some other less valuable or worthless material they could hold all of the valuable stuff and have even more control over the citizens. And when the government needed (or wanted) more money they could just stamp out more "non-precious" coins.

But the government knew that to keep its citizens using and valuing these "non-precious" coins they would have to hold something precious in inventory or under their control (gold, emeralds, salt, oil, etc.). The government had to discover and collect these precious items from within their own boundaries. That's a lot of work and the item in quest may not be readily available within their own boundaries. It was much easier for the government to send out their army to invade another civilization—kill them or enslave them—and take their valuables and precious materials.

Money didn't only give the government more control of citizens; it gave people a means of exchange. It expanded their options and choices. That meant I wouldn't have to stock up on only dried figs. As long as I had some recognized money I could buy a few dried figs now; hold on to the remainder of my money and wait until I found a merchant who had fresh figs. I didn't have to worry about my money rotting, so I could save my money and use it in the future to buy other items that were seasonal, like apples, peaches, citrus, nuts, berries or something that was recently butchered or a single live chicken. Money—as a medium of trading—gave me choices.

Money also allowed me to travel. I didn't have to carry a half ton of tin or figs with me. I could have a pouch of recognized coins, jewels or gold dust hidden in my loincloth. I could go from city to city or country to country. Money and mutually accepted precious valuables enabled the start of international trade long before the dawn of the internet.

As governments and political systems evolved, different regions had different kinds of "money." As people acquired more money, along with different kinds of money from other countries, they needed a place to store it or exchange it. This brought the advent of "banks" and "the money changers" into existence.

Somewhere around A.D. 900-1000, the Chinese empire allowed for what was called open banking. A bank would store your valuables and issue you "notes" (paper money) backed by your valuables and you could use those bank-issued notes to buy and trade with. Those notes could then be redeemed for your stored valuables but only at the issuing bank. So this still limited the value of these notes and limited trading among different communities and countries. Your "bank note" might be credible and valuable in your hometown, but if I have to travel 300 miles (on a very slow and smelly ox) to redeem your bank's or city's notes, then they're not worth much value to me. That's where the "money changers" came in. I could sell you my product for your "notes" and then exchange those notes (for a fee) with a "money changer."

During the 18th and 19th centuries, citizens of the United States extended their hold across the new continent. People still needed to trade, but there was no mutually recognized money. Pieces of gold and gold dust were used as a means to buy what you wanted. Gold is heavy and difficult to give change back. So independent banks would hold and protect your gold and issue you their notes that you could spend against your gold.

As more and more banks became involved they all had different notes and the actual value of their notes varied. And if a trader couldn't use or redeem your bank note it was worthless to both of you. A "note" from a bank in Louisiana wouldn't do you much good in Colorado. After the civil war the U.S. Government stepped in. Through legal decrees they created "Central Banking." That meant that any community, city, state or country within their domain could use the same notes (and coins), issued by the government, as a common means of trade. The idea was to standardize value and make trading easier among their inhabitants (and collect taxes on trades). A standardized U.S. dollar could now be accepted in New York, Illinois, Louisiana or California.

Here is not the place to debate the correctness of the U.S. central banking system, whether it is corrupt, or whether the change from the gold standard to the fiat standard was a scam perpetrated by the government. Regardless of how you feel about these things, none of that should deter you from realizing and accepting that **this is the system we have in place now**. What we currently recognize as "money" (regardless of it being U.S. Dollars, English Pounds, Euro, Yen, etc.) is how we buy and sell things today. Money will continue to evolve and what we know as currency today *may* be worthless in the future. But don't let that stop you from valuing a dollar now.

Yes, people still continue to barter, albeit within certain limits, and people continue to buy gold, silver, jewels and other precious valuables. But those valuables are first purchased with a currency, then saved and stored for exchange into whatever currency may eventually be needed in the future. And regardless of how much gold, silver or precious jewels you have, you still need *tradable money* for most of life's purchases. You can't go grocery shopping or pay a utility bill with a bar of gold. Life requires some means of mutually accepted tradable money. Even if your credit or debit card is based against your gold holdings, when the bill is due, some of the gold you own is sold (at current market value) and converted into a mutually accepted currency.

At this writing there has emerged another type of currency called "Bitcoin." The idea behind bitcoin is that the free market establishes the value of its numeric quantification. The U.S. government doesn't accept or acknowledge bitcoin as a currency. You can't go to your local grocery store and buy food with bitcoins. Most stores do not accept bitcoins as payment but a few online retailers do. So if you want to buy a car, make a loan payment or pay your taxes with bitcoins you still need to find a bitcoin trader that is willing to exchange your bitcoins for U.S. currency. And the "value" of a bitcoin is established by bitcoin traders. At this writing *I believe* that bitcoins are a novelty item, but who knows what the concept may lead to and evolve into?

I personally can't foresee the use of money ever going away. I also can't foresee a standardized world currency ever happening. Even with open world markets and trade as we have now, money is still converted into the currency of your geographical location. You may have purchased my book with Euros, Yen or Australian Dollars, but my account was credited with U.S. dollars. Like it or not, money is here to stay. Our current currencies may change or disappear, but something will always represent "value" which will allow it to be traded. It would pretty much require the end of civilization as we know it for "money" to disappear.

Many questions arise about what money can and can't buy. That is subjective to each individual and I'll leave that for further discussion in a later chapter. There is also the question of how much money is enough? Again, that is different for each individual and will be discussed in a later chapter.

The point here is to understand that—whether you like it or not—money is how we transact, feed and clothe ourselves, value ourselves by earning wages and keep score. Keeping score doesn't mean life is a contest to see who can collect the most points. Keeping score is a matter of knowing how many points are coming in so you know how many points you have and how many you can spend.

Money—as an object—is worthless until something is done with it (spent, invested or leveraged). Money is inert, people aren't. Money is not evil; people do evil things for money. Wealth is not bad, greed of wealth is bad. Money can make your life easier, afford you to be more altruistic and help you to help others get ahead. It can also ruin your life, bring out the worst in someone and make relationships far more complicated.

There is no doubt that money is important and it can be a painful existence if you don't have any. Money isn't everything—it's the only thing. Without it you can't provide for yourself or for the people you are responsible for or care about. Without money you limit your choices in life. But money is just a modern-day means of barter and nothing more.

Even though I just said that money is simply our modern-day way of bartering, money stirs up all kinds of emotions and behaviors within people. Here are some of emotions and reactions involved with "money."

Money corrupts: Wealth can change a person, sometimes for the better, sometimes for the worse. The lack of money corrupts some people's morals and they steal, cheat, participate in unlawful activities and even commit murder. Money can motivate people to behave and do the opposite of what they normally would without its influence.

Possessing money can bring you results and conditions that you didn't desire or hadn't anticipated. All kinds of rats will come out of the woodwork when you have money. These rats want you to lend them or give them your money. Some will falsely befriend you in hopes of accessing your money. Some people who obtain money and wealth will become uppity and arrogant, feeling that their peers are below them because "those people" haven't achieved wealth like they have.

Money can corrupt, but it doesn't have to. Money can motivate you away from corruption to do good things. Some of those things might be to work harder, work smarter, expand your education, reduce expenses, improve living conditions for yourself, family and friends. You may be driven to become benevolent and help as many people as you can. Money doesn't automatically corrupt.

Temptation: Money causes you to think differently. There is the temptation to spend it—every last penny of it that you have. And there are temptations to do anything (illegal or immoral) simply because you want more of it. Temptation will come at the most peculiar and inconvenient times and can cause a moral person to do some crazy things to acquire money, a logical person to make bad decisions or a conservative investor to take foolish risks. That's why it's good to have a savings of money as a safety net—a safety net helps to offset and dampen the power of temptation.

Self-doubt and self-pity: Feelings of self-doubt happen when you think you don't deserve to live well or don't deserve to have a comfortable amount of money. This feeling hits when you think you're overpaid for your job or position. (Don't laugh, many people do and have felt this way.) Comparing your income, wealth or material possessions against your neighbor's is also self-doubt. These comparisons and self-doubt can drive a person to overspend or corrupt themselves so they can "keep up with the Jones's."

Self-pity is when you feel you are entitled to have more money than you do. You might feel underpaid, undervalued or you feel you deserve to have as much as someone else. Self-pity can also drive a person to corruption, "I deserve to have more. He's got plenty so I'll take some of his."

Self-pity can also fuel feelings of self-doubt. "I'm broke, I'm worthless, I have no skills or talent. Add to that I'm ugly and stupid to boot. I'll never have money." Feelings like this can wipe out all motivation to better your own existence. It can become a self-fulfilling prophecy.

Anger: You might get angry at "wealthy people" or at money itself. Angry because you don't have enough of it or because you realize that your quest for money drives you to do things that aren't pleasant or go against your moral fiber. It's not uncommon to hate people who *appear* to have money or wealth. But the truth is those people you hate may be more in hock than you. They may be in debt up to their eyeballs and have to work 50 to 60 hours a week at a miserable job just so they *appear* wealthy to everyone else. You also may not know how they achieved their wealth. They may be moral, honest, hardworking people. They may have studied, struggled, scrimped, sacrificed and saved to get to where they are today.

Anger has also been used to motivate many out of poverty. "I'm better than this. I will rise above this and I vow to make my life better." That type of person may become an entrepreneur, a business owner or pursue higher education to make themselves a highly valued and highly paid employee. They put in the time, dedication and self-control to honestly earn their wealth. Then they become one of the "rich people" that others like to hate.

Guilt: You might feel guilty because you don't earn enough money to support yourself or your family comfortably. Or you might feel guilty for doing well while some of your family members or friends struggle to make ends meet.

Feelings of financial guilt can be overcome—but only by you and through you taking action. If you feel guilty because you don't earn enough, what can YOU do to make yourself more valuable to the market? If you feel guilty about always being broke (even though you earn well), what can YOU do to pare down frivolous and unnecessary expenses? If you feel guilty because you do better than your family or friends you can become more benevolent. You don't have to give away all of your money to relatives and friends, you can be a mentor and show others how to improve their own lot.

Frustration: You might feel frustrated because you're always a little short on money. You might feel frustrated because no matter how hard you try you just can't get ahead of your bills, save or earn as much as you would like to. In most cases there is a simple and logical reason. Do you live by a budget? Do you even know how much you spend and on what? Are you living within your means? Are you living the life of a hyper consumer with high-status stuff just to impress people or keep up with others? Do you have an honest understanding of the value of your marketable skills? What can YOU do to increase your income and/or pare down your expenses? Spending less and spending wisely within a budget is the easiest way to give yourself a pay raise. We'll go over this in chapter #7.

Sadness and depression: Sadness and depression can stem from any of the above mentioned emotions. Believe it or not, sadness and depression can also happen to wealthy people. They thought that money would bring them happiness but it hasn't because they are still a slave to money. They have more stuff, but they might have more bills and more debt because they spend most, all or more money than they earn. With all the money they earn and spend they may not be any less lonely, no happier or financially secure.

Along with all the emotions that are stirred up by money, there may be unintended, unwanted and unanticipated changes and conditions that occur. In these next few paragraphs I'll focus on what may (or may not), happen to you as you acquire and accumulate wealth.

27

The changing or dissolution of friendships and relationships: Some friendships and relationships will end as a result of you obtaining money. Many of the emotions I just covered may be felt or held against you. Family and friends can become jealous of your improved existence. Some will feel as if you should share your wealth with them, "With all your money you should pay for dinner," or "help me out." And if you won't, then they don't want to be your friend anymore (good riddance). Your romantic relationship or marriage may become strained. "Look at all the money you earn. You should spend more on me."

Relationships—especially marriages—can become volatile and unhealthy when financial values are vastly different. If you're a saver and your spouse/partner has an attitude of "spend, spend, spend" then you're going to have problems. You don't have to have the exact same values towards earning, spending and saving, but similar goals will help the relationship blossom into something fun and rewarding for both of you.

A person who has wealth, and either flaunts it or it is discovered, can make that person attractive to others. As long as you have money—and spend it—parasites will hang around. Once the money's gone or turned off, so are they. If you're in a relationship or married, don't be surprised if someone from outside your marriage tries to draw you away from it. This is simply the other person engaging in "survival of the fittest," by trying to snare a wealthy, good provider. (Don't write me off as bitter, cynical or untrusting because of what I just said. Your partner or future partner may be nothing like this. But the fact **is** that money and wealth can attract people who aren't interested in you—they're interested in your money. Just be aware of this.)

You may also fall prey to feelings of superiority and look down on your "poor" friends because they can't keep up with you. You may end up dumping your bourgeois friends and go hang out with the wealthy people. That's your choice. But then you'll only be supporting the heading of this segment: **The changing or**

dissolution of friendships and relationships and reinforcing my statement of "money changes everything."

Unspent money in your pocket: This is a new dilemma for many people. If you've never had extra money available you won't know what to do with it. A lot of people feel like they should spend it on material items. Go ahead, but burning through newfound wealth won't help towards the development of sustained wealth. I won't bore you with the statistics of how rapidly second-generation inherited money is often burned through. But believe me, it happens all the time.

Excess money and wealth create a curious conundrum. You have extra money so why not spend it? I can understand that mindset and I certainly wouldn't fault someone for thinking that way. But that is not how you build and sustain wealth. And excess money can lead to destructive excess. If you earn more you can afford to party more. You can afford higher quality and higher quantities of booze and drugs. But if you do more booze and drugs you run the risk of becoming addicted and running out of savings and crippling your ability to earn at the same high level. Then you're back to being broke again, only now you also have a substance dependency problem, and that would really suck.

Summary: The purpose of this chapter is to get you thinking about what money really is. I believe that when you really understand what money is—just a means to trade, barter and transact—it becomes less mysterious, scary or sacred. Don't be afraid of money or afraid of numbers. The best thing you can do for yourself is understand and accept what money is and then try to get the most utility out of your money.

What is money worksheet:

Do you feel like you have a good understanding of what money is? What do YOU think it is and why?_____

Do you feel like you are a slave to money?_____

What emotions do you feel when you think about money?_____

Are you comfortable with those emotions or do they unsettle you?_____

What can you do to make yourself more comfortable with the subject of money?_____

What can you do to better understand the power of money?_____

Have you ever known anyone who *changed* because of money? For the better or the worse?_____

Do you think YOU would *change* because of money? For the better or for the worse?_____

Chapter #2

What is wealth?

Assumptions about money.

"When you don't know what you want you're susceptible to accept anything that comes your way."

Money is so important in our daily life that it's difficult to not become a slave to it. Money is strange that way because as you acquire more of it you would think that you'd no longer be its slave, but you can become dependent on it and addicted to it. You aren't necessarily addicted to the money itself, but you become dependent and addicted to what money can bring you. Like an addict, your mind can become fixated on it. And taking the addict example a step further, your body can go through physical sensations when you see money, think about money, hold money in your hands, acquire money and lose money.

Your socioeconomic background, religious background, peers, culture and geographical location have an influence on how you feel about money and wealth and what you consider as wealth. Who you hang out with and who you identify with, admire or model yourself after have an influence on your feelings toward money and wealth. If your peers idolize drug dealers or gaining money through criminal activity then you'll probably do the same. If you see conspicuous and flashy showings of material possessions as wealth, you'll probably want the same. If your peers are computer geeks or craftsmen of some sort, your view of money will be different than in the prior group. Breaking away from your peer group can be costly—financially, socially and emotionally— that's why many people stay right where they are geographically and financially.

Some people grow up in poverty and never worry about money, they figure they'll never have it or don't deserve it. Those people can actually be happier, more giving and far more pleasant than someone who earns a lot but is burdened by high debt, struggling to constantly show everyone how wealthy they are through their possessions. Some people grow up in affluence and develop a sense of entitlement, a sense that they should always have plenty of money, even if it's at someone else's expense. A poor youth may grow up vowing to never be poor again, work hard and do well for himself and his family. Whereas a child from a wealthy family may walk away from all of the material trappings money affords and exist on bare minimums in adulthood. Many people and conditions will influence your feelings about money, but you personally must decide how you will act towards and behave with money.

Money is a logical and empirical article because mathematical facts govern money. $20 from $100 leaves you with $80. A 5% return on $500 is $25. Because mathematical facts govern money, conventional economic theorists take the position that people will be logical with their money, but they aren't. This doesn't mean that people are wrong or stupid. You buy things that you desire or buy what fills the needs within your choice range, and your choice range limited by how much money you have or can borrow. People want to own and do nice things so they may make illogical purchases. But illogical to whom? Illogical to the person who makes the purchase or to an economist?

Let me give you some examples of purchases people make. In my examples these people live in the same city but come from vastly different socio-economic backgrounds and distinctly different parts of the city. I would like you to decide whose purchases are logical or illogical and what you would do in their situation.

My friend Bernard lives in what most people would call "the poor part of town." The majority of the people who live in his neighborhood are renters, only a few own their home. But there are some nice cars in that neighborhood. They're not all new cars either, some are 10 and 20 years old but sure do look fine. Bernard has an older car and he takes good care of it. He was able to get a bargain on some spinning chrome hubcaps that cost him only $600 for all 4 of them. (It was a private transaction.) Brand new these hubcaps would have cost around $1,200 for all 4. Bernard did a few side jobs to earn some extra cash, asked his uncle if he could be a little late for his portion of rent and bought the hubcaps. He still owes for his part of the rent but he'll pay that next week when he gets his check. But hey, his ride looks awesome.

An economist or someone from outside Bernard's neighborhood and social circle may think that his purchase of spinning chrome hubcaps was "illogical" and being late on rent is irresponsible. But if the item and the act of making the purchase makes Bernard happy, and his chrome hubcaps makes him look cool and galvanizes him among his peers, then he has gotten **utility** out of his money and *that* makes logical sense to him because that's the world he lives in.

My opinion is that Bernard should have paid his rent on time, made a down payment towards the hubcaps, asked the seller to hold them and paid the balance next week. But that's not how private business deals work in Bernard's neighborhood. In Bernard's world if you want something you pay cash for it now. Bernard could have easily seen his down payment money and the seller disappear, so he had to pay for them in full. Besides, he's been late on his rent before and his uncle never kicked him out. So I don't see Bernard as stupid or illogical for making the purchase. I understand his motive for buying the hubcaps—to improve his status among his neighbors and social circle. However, if Bernard was saving money for college, then I would say the purchase of spinning hubcaps was definitely a *foolish* use of his limited money. The money he spent on hubcaps is gone and no matter how cool they look they won't make him any smarter or any more employable like attending college will (or I should say "would have," because now he doesn't have $600 to apply towards tuition).

Reading my story about Bernard may make you think he has a low income or an illegal income and lives in the ghetto. Do we know? Did I say any of those things? In fact, he works very hard at his job in construction and earns a modest income. He lives in a neighborhood where the houses are old and not very expensive, but most of the residents have pride and keep their yards clean. Bernard owns his car outright (he bought it used), and has no monthly car payment to make. Don't assume anything about Bernard. Assumptions can turn into prejudice.

But let's say that Bernard does live in a rough part of town and he does earn his income from his job in the "Recreational Services Industry." His neighbors, family and peers think spinning hubcaps are a status symbol, so buying them was logical. But Bernard has plans to attend college someday and "earn an honest living and get out of this shit-hole neighborhood and lifestyle forever." His purchase of spinning hubcaps doesn't get him any closer to that dream. I say "dream" because if it were a "goal" he would have a plan, a budget and use his money more wisely, regardless of the fact that his line of work is part of an illegal business. His street education and business savvy may help him become a legitimate—and profitable—business owner someday even if he doesn't attend college.

If you *assume* that all people who live in poor neighborhoods are financially stupid and are influenced by their peers, then let me tell you about Jenny and her husband Pete. Both Jenny and Pete are well educated, hard working high-earners who live in a very nice neighborhood with high property taxes. They have a huge mortgage payment every month and they each have leased vehicles with monthly payments. Let's not get into how much their boat payments are or how much credit card debt they carry monthly, oh, and student loans don't count because they can always keep deferring payments or just default on them. Anyway...

Jenny and Pete paid over $5,000 for a hot tub. Why did they get a hot tub? Some friends of theirs had one. They thought a hot tub would be fun and a sign of status. They figured they would use their hot tub all the time entertaining neighbors and guests. (They didn't consider how much it costs to entertain friends and guests—snobby wines and cheese aren't cheap you know.) They also thought (told themselves or were told by the salesman), that a hot tub would increase the resale value of their home, even though they have no plans of selling their home anytime soon.

So what happened? They didn't use their hot tub as often as they thought they would and Pete spent more time doing maintenance then relaxing in it. They live in Wisconsin and the hot tub has to always be covered so it needed to be cleaned and chemically treated regularly. And in Wisconsin it needs to be heated year-round, whether you're using it or not. After 3 years of monthly payments, when they finally had it paid off, they decided to sell it. The hot tub was 3 years old, hardly ever used, in like-new condition, had all sorts of fancy features and fountains and bubbly things. Know how much they got for it? **$300**. There isn't much demand for hot tubs in Wisconsin. And if you live in Wisconsin and you can afford to put a hot tub on your deck you're probably going to buy a brand new one. "Used hot tub! What would the neighbors think?"

Jenny and her husband are both high-earners, so they could afford the down payment and qualified for the 36 month loan payments, along with the chemicals and ridiculous annual cost to heat a hot tub in Wisconsin. If you add the cost to heat it to the $5000+ purchase price you come to a conservative total of $5750. Had Jenny and her husband put that money into a conservative mutual fund or even a bank savings account, they would have well over $6000 right now. Did they really get $6000 worth of enjoyment and status out of their hot tub? I doubt it.

This is just an example of how *wealthy people* and *poor people* buy stuff because of peer influence. The story of Jenny and Pete shows how *wealthy people* can be hurt more through peer pressure and buying "stuff" because they have a higher income to pay for it, without considering how much it's really going to cost them in the long run. It will cost them WELL over $6000 because that money is gone and it won't be earning them interest, dividends or capital appreciation over the next 20 years.

The story of Bernard is something I fictionalized, but I personally do know people like Bernard because I was one of them. The story of Jenny and Pete is real. I do know them personally and they are very nice people. They're smart and hardworking but not in good financial shape. Bernard, as well as Jenny and Pete, are living paycheck-to-paycheck. Jenny and Pete earn a lot more money than Bernard does but they have no net worth to show for it, other than a little equity in their home, which is unrealized, unless they apply for a home equity loan, which they may have already done. Sadly, all Jenny and Pete have to show for all their hard work and high income is debt. Whereas Bernard has no debt and if he really needed money he could sell his spinning chrome hubcaps for about the same amount ($300) that Jenny and Pete got for their $5,000 hot tub.

Between Jenny and her husband and Bernard, who do you think is more financially savvy? Who do you think will have more financial problems in the future? Jenny and Pete currently have more earning potential than Bernard, but they also have the potential to get themselves further into debt. Who do you think is more likely to eventually file for bankruptcy? Who do you think will never break their cycle of 'living broke'?

Both of them (Jenny and her husband and Bernard) need to change their financial thinking and their financial behavior if they want to break their 'living broke' cycle. Jenny and Pete have a head start here. They have stable, high paying jobs and with a bit of self-control and budgeting they could turn their situation around and begin building wealth or at least build a safety net. Bernard has a tougher and longer road ahead of him if he wants to become a high-earner or business owner, but that doesn't mean he can't or won't do it.

Then there are some people, both the wealthy and the poor, who are not influenced by their peers and who actually make choices with budgetary limits and constraints in mind (this being an unheard of or unfathomable concept to hyper-spenders). This type of person has specific categories written down for purchases and allocates (budgets) specific dollar amounts that they are going to spend on items within the categories. They don't do this to torture themselves or to live like paupers in a substandard existence. They eat well, enjoy fine products, own reliable cars, go on vacations. They pretty much own and do everything that hyper-spenders own and do, except they don't hyper-spend and go into debt. They budget how much they will spend on food, automobiles, a home, vacation, etc. They know how much money is coming in and going out and they save or invest the rest. Of course they would enjoy driving the latest model Mercedes or a brand new Lexus, but a clean, 3-year old used Ford Fiesta will serve their utility purposes just fine right now. And who knows, they may even buy a Lexus sometime in the future when they feel they have built up enough of a financial safety net, but it'll be a "pre-owned" Lexus. I admit that I do have some well off friends who only buy brand new cars, but I also know that they keep their cars for 10 to 20 years. They get **full utility** out of their brand new car purchase.

I find it interesting that if it weren't for people buying brand new cars every 3 years, that they can't afford, and high-earners leasing luxury cars that they have to return early because they can't make the payments, financially savvy people wouldn't have any quality used cars to buy or find luxury used cars at rock bottom prices.

The choices people make (not just financially), usually stem from what and who they identify with along with peer influences. Adults are just as, if not more influenced by their peers than teenagers are. In fact, peer influence can be more dangerous among adults because adults typically have more money to spend, make larger purchases and can go further into debt than a teenager.

Assumptions about money and wealth:

Most of us *assume* that money will make us happy. Well, it certainly doesn't hurt, but sometimes it does hurt us. I'll go over that concept in greater detail in Chapter #7. Right now, let's look at some of the assumptions people have about money, wealth, spending decisions and investing.

Money: "Money isn't everything." Well, try living without it. Like it or not you need money to survive, unless you live in the wilderness and survive off the land eating bugs and berries. If that's the case you wouldn't be reading this book. So let's agree that you do need money to live in our current society. You can live a very Spartan lifestyle, do a lot of bartering and trading of services, but you'll still need money to buy even the basics. At the very minimum, someone else used money to buy what you are bartering your services for. Money is necessary. So why live without it?

Wealth: All rich people are not evil. All poor people are not lazy. Almost every successful person has had at least one failure that you **aren't aware of**. Wealthy people are often *assumed* to be selfish and greedy. Some are but many aren't. Just because a wealthy person doesn't simply give their money away to anyone who asks for it doesn't mean their selfish or greedy. A wealthy person can be quite generous by offering opportunity. Wealthy people can own businesses that sell other people products at a fair price. They offer the opportunity to work for them, the opportunity to invest in them or partner up with them.

So while every wealthy person or semi-wealthy person may not be a philanthropist, they offer the masses (me included), an opportunity to have a job and earn an income either by them being high-spending consumers or business owners. Without wealthy business owners we wouldn't have many places to work. (I'm using "wealthy business owner" in a joking sense. Many business owners are struggling more than their employees to make ends meet, or they have scrimped, saved and sacrificed to develop their successful business.) Owning a business is a high risk, but with that risk can come some great rewards.

The difference between "High-Income" and "Wealth."
Many people *assume* that if someone earns a high-income and has a lot of flashy status material objects they must be wealthy. Earning a high-income doesn't automatically equate to being wealthy or building wealth. Many high-income earners spend their entire annual income—or worse yet, they have created more debt for themselves by the end of the year.

Someone who nets $100,000 a year and burns through it may have a lot of pretty toys to show off and may have had a blast spending it, but they are likely to have NO tangible assets or wealth accumulation to show for it. If they lose their job they can always pawn their $3,000 watch for .25 cents on the dollar (or less), but they won't get .25 cents on the dollar for their tailored suites, fancy carpeting and flamboyant furniture. And if they do have to sell those items that means they no longer have them to wear and show off.

But a person who nets $18,000 a year and is able to put $1,200 ($100 per month) into a 401(K), IRA or mutual fund is wealthier than the high earner. After 5 years the low earner will have amassed about $6,500 (probably more) in their retirement account and the high-earner will have amassed zero.

Now $6,500 may not sound like much, but the low-earner can survive on that for quite a while if they get laid off—without having to sell any of their possessions or change their standard of existence—until they find employment again. Whereas the high earner **will** have to sell stuff (that's if they own it, otherwise it's just repossessed), and they're going to have to make some dramatic changes in their life and standard of existence if they can't quickly find another high-paying job. And if they have no savings—only debt—they don't have seed money to start their own business or get a business loan (due to their high personal debt).

If you *assume* that earning a lot of money and spending most of it means you're wealthy, you will never become genuinely wealthy. Many people believe that showy status items are an indicator of wealth. It's okay if you also believe this because most people don't grasp or understand what genuine wealth is—but **you** can and will.

> **Wealth building and genuine wealth are a way of life. You spend less than you earn and you save or invest the rest. You eliminate debt, build yourself a financial safety net and you set money aside to be used in the future. That is genuine wealth.**

How much you need and what amount you consider as 'wealthy' will be discussed in chapter #7. But starting NOW, I would like you to begin building wealth and build yourself a financial safety net because: **Fortunes can change rapidly.**

So much of our life is out of our control or we simply aren't aware of what's going on behind the scenes. The weather turns extremely hot or extremely cold. There's a drought or a flood somewhere. Suddenly the price of food goes up, the price of gasoline goes up and the price of utilities goes up. These are all conditions you can't control. Other events such as changes in laws, political changes, economic changes, social changes, new innovations or world turmoil may cause your employer to close shop or eliminate your job. As the saying goes: "Shit happens." And sadly, it happens to good, hardworking people who don't deserve it—and don't have a financial safety net.

You're not dumb, gullible or being played for a fool when unforeseen events occur. You can't expect that you'll see everything coming your way or that you should have been able to "read the writing on the wall." You only have so much time to research and absorb data. There's only so much information you can know about your company, its plans, its sales successes, the weather, social and geopolitical changes. What's even harder is determining whether the data your reading or being told is true or not. And there's only so much you can personally do to act on the data, let alone have a direct influence on large-scale conditions. What you can control (within limits), is how much money you're willing to spend, what you're willing to buy and how much you can save towards building your own wealth and security.

Spending decisions and budgets: People don't have every piece of data to compare and make the best decision. Simply put, people don't always make the best buying decisions due to lack of data, social and advertising influence, peer pressure, lack of self-control or their own innumeracy. A person may know exactly how much they earn in a year but they have no solid concept of how much they spend in a year or what they spent it on. Financially stable people (both wealthy and poor) live by following a budget. Actual budgets and budgeting will be gone over in the next chapter.

It is also commonly *assumed* that people buy something because they chose it; meaning that they either needed it or desired it. But people often spend money on things that are bad for them (that's what alcoholics, drug addicts, gambling addicts, addicted smokers, clothes hoarders, and hyper-spenders do). And people don't always choose something because it was *their* choice. They may have been influenced by a salesperson, advertising, social status, peers or other unseen factors. This is not to infer that people are stupid, gullible, weak or always make poor choices. But many choices are based on *assumptions*.

Tipping is a good example of an *assumption* about spending. If I go to an elegant restaurant and my final bill is $120 (for 4 people) I will not automatically leave an $18 tip (15%). If we received poor service, I may leave less or leave no tip at all. But if we received great service I may leave a $25 tip. The same applies if you have a 2-for-1 meal coupon or go for the $1.99 special at the casino, 15% gratuity is a "rule of thumb" and an *assumption*. You don't have to tip on a percentage of the final bill. If you get a discount meal and the bill is $9 it's a bit ridiculous (if not insulting to a good server), to leave a $1.35 tip (15% of the bill). Tip on the quality of service you received. As a side note, if you can't afford to leave a good tip then you probably can't afford to be dining out and you should be cooking or entertaining at home.

Investing: People *assume* that investments will make them wealthy. Every investment **will not** be profitable. But I can tell you this much; If you're money is not invested in something, you are **guaranteed** that you **will not make any money**. Money sitting on your dresser or stuffed in your mattress does not earn you more money. You can buy precious metals or gems, hide them and hope they increase in value, but they may not. And even if they do increase in value, they aren't of any use until you sell them (or leverage against them) and turn them into spendable money. Investing instruments will be covered in chapter #11.

Material items are a sign of wealth: People *assume* that if someone drives a luxury car, wears tons of jewelry, lives in a giant home and has a lot of toys that they are wealthy. They might be, but they also might be broke, living paycheck-to-paycheck. The luxury car might be leased and they hold no equity in it. Their boat, camper, pool, furniture and jewelry may be all financed through loans. They have a lot of stuff but they don't actually own any of it. All their stuff just shows that they spend a lot of money—and it's not even their own money.

This is not to say that these people aren't enjoying their life, even if they are in debt. And let's not *assume* that someone who drives a luxury car or lives in a nice home doesn't own it. When you have built genuine wealth (and a financial safety net), you are in a position to afford nice things and those nice things are rarely financed through loans. Wealthy people can afford and do buy nice things.

I'm not trying to confuse you or sound inconsistent about wealth and possessing high-status material items. My work in substance counseling puts me in contact with a wide variety of people and lifestyles. I get to know a lot of private personal and financial details about people. I have found that when someone has to "show" that they're wealthy—they aren't. The genuinely wealthy don't need to show off and are often humble when they do have obvious high-status objects. Genuinely wealthy people don't have to brag or impress. In fact, they often try to hide from public view how much wealth they really do have. They do this to practice humility and self-control. It's also how they protect themselves from parasites and conmen. If people *think* you're wealthy or know that you're genuinely wealthy, you will be inundated with pleas for assistance, loans, purchases and the ever popular "once in a lifetime investment opportunity." Accumulation of wealth is the first step, after that it's preservation of your wealth.

What do you want?

At this point I want to ask you, "What do YOU want out of your money?" Early in this book is the time to think about this question. As we get further we'll look at what you think wealth is, how much wealth you want, in what manner you want to hold your wealth, the difference between purchases and investments. We'll consider what is good debt and bad debt and when you might want to carry debt.

For right now I would like you to think about what YOU want out of money. You need to know and see—in concrete terminology and form—**exactly** what you want to gain, have or do with your money. I would like you to write out **exactly** what you *want* and *don't want* out of money. Knowing what you *don't want* is equally as important as knowing what you *do want*. In fact, knowing what you don't want may actually be more important to some of you.

You may want money or to earn a high income, but you don't want to dedicate your every waking moment to working. You will have to make exchanges then. Higher income typically means more time at work or more time advancing your skills and making yourself more valuable through extra education. This will all require time. Are you willing to make that exchange?

You may prefer to spend time with family, your children or enjoying the things you can afford to buy. Spending more time with children or at leisure means you will have less time to earn money at work. That means you will have to make your money work for you. You'll have to spend less and save more in investments.

You may **not want** to have multiple payments that must be paid every month. You might earn a lot of money and have a good credit rating, so you hyper-spend on material possessions and then you have a zillion monthly payments for stuff you don't have time to use. Or you're always nervous about making all of the various monthly payments. At that point money isn't fun. It's not fun to become a slave to money. You may want wealth and a high income but you **don't want** to become a slave to your stuff , creditors or money. You will have to make concessions and exchanges then.

"What you *want* out of money" and "What you *don't want* out of money" are completely selfish questions and they will be some of the most important questions you will ask yourself. It can help you decide if you're willing to make the exchange of working more hours to earn more money. It may help you reevaluate your current job and current level of education. You may discover that you're happy right where you're at. Once you have answered these two questions in detail, you then have the *core* of what you will want to do with your money and better understand if you're driven by money. It will also make saving money a bit easier; in fact, it may make it a fun goal.

Is this tedious, time consuming and mentally taxing? Yes. You're going to have to really think and be introspective. You'll have to think about yourself and about the other people in your life. If you have a spouse or children, you will have to take them into consideration. If you have debts, responsibilities or any other obligations that you're accountable for, you'll have to take those into consideration as well. Is this something that you'll have to do only once? No. Your lists and goals will always be evolving. As you accomplish things on your list, you'll want to continuously update your list because your desires and needs will change as your personal and financial situation changes.

As you undertake this exercise, your enthusiasm about your financial future might increase because you're thinking that everything will now finally start taking shape and things will work out in your life. Here's where I need to remind you that you might not get everything you want out of money. I'm not trying to be a downer or sound depressing. The reality is that some things that you want out of money won't happen. Just because you want something, make an intelligent plan to accomplish it and do all the right activities to make it happen, doesn't mean it will happen. The best laid plans don't always work out. And if your expectations are too high or unrealistic, you'll be setting yourself up for disappointment.

Your *wants* need to be realistic. That doesn't mean you don't dream big, but you have to consider whether your wants are *feasible* and *probable*. Let me explain feasible and probable in an example. Let's say that one of my *wants* is to buy a mansion in Beverly Hills. That means I would have to somehow get a lot of money, then live and work in California. Living and working in California is feasible, but it's not very probable that I would ever earn enough money to afford a mansion in Beverly Hills. So my realistic goal should be: I want to buy a nice little home somewhere near the coast in Southern California. Now that's feasible and more probable, but that's only if I move to California, have stable employment and find a place that I can afford.

Let me give another example. You *want* to earn $100,000 a year, but if you work in an assembly plant or as a cashier in a retail store that's not going to happen. Your income is limited by the maximum pay your position allows—therefore both probability and feasibility of earning $100,000 a year at your job are wiped off

45

the table. However, if you advanced your education and exhibited leadership skills you may qualify for a managerial or supervisory job, leading to a $50,000 a year position. That is feasible and only more probable if you do the work to further your value to the marketplace.

But you're dead set on earning $100,000 a year. What can YOU do to make this feasible and more probable? What talents do you have? What talents or knowledge must you develop to make yourself that valuable to the marketplace? Do you even have the mental capacity to become knowledgeable and skilled in a job that pays that kind of money? I'm not trying to insult you or take the wind out of you sails, but is it even feasible that you could ever earn that kind of money? As painful as it may be, you need to be brutally honest with yourself. I may want to make a million dollars as a professional athlete, but my physical limitations make it infeasible and impossible that it could ever happen, so I must pursue other careers that are feasible and probable for me to successfully perform in.

If you really want to make the most out of this exercise you will have to do some thinking and writing work. You will construct two separate lists. One will be titled "What I *want* out of money" and the other will be titled "What I *don't want* out of money." On each of your lists you'll make two columns. On the left will be the **goal or desire** and on the right will be a brief description of **what you need to do and how you need to behave to make it happen**.

You want concrete statements or goals, followed by a brief description of the activities that you will have to perform to achieve those goals. You'll also want to periodically review your list, track your progress, accomplishments and your success rate. Is this a lot of tedious work? Yes. But *great things in life don't happen by ambiguous efforts and random activities*. They happen due to focused thought, focused effort and concrete plans.

You are the only person who knows what you want. Don't be influenced by advertisers, celebrities, neighbors, family or anyone else telling you what you *should* want. Here are a few sample goals to get you thinking:

> I want to spend more quality time with my kids, spouse, boyfriend or girlfriend, relatives, family, friends, whoever is important to you in your life. I want to be able to pay my monthly bills without worry. I want to save up money for a new car. I want to further my education and get a new job. I want to take my family on a vacation to Florida or wherever. I want to move into a larger or smaller home or apartment. I want to pay off my mortgage or save enough for a down payment on a house. I want to start an IRA. I want to save a certain amount of money every month towards my retirement. I want to be able to afford the kinds of food I like. I want to afford to be involved in a certain hobby or sport. I want to have less stress worrying about money.

Now let me give you some examples for your DON'T want list:

> I don't want to always be hounded by my friends or family asking me for loans or to pay off their debt. I don't want to be involved in "get rich quick" schemes and always chasing an easy dollar. I don't want to be a slave to my stuff, creditors and earning money. I don't want to feel the need to impress people through how much I can spend. I don't want to always be in debt or constantly increasing it. I don't want to spend money on useless things or things that I can't afford. I don't want to spend my life working trying to get my hands on more money.

Again, these are just samples to get you thinking. I suggest you write out your own unique *wants* and *don't wants* and then describe what action or behavior is required to accomplish each of them. For instance if you want to take your family on a vacation, where will this vacation be? When do you want to go in this vacation? How long will the vacation last? How much money will you need to pay for it? Will you earn extra money or reduce expenses? Where will you physically save the money so it's available when it's time for the vacation?

Please spend the time to make your own lists or to at least think about them. The time you spend is for your own benefit. Please do this for yourself. If you don't know what you want you'll never know what you could have accomplished.

I am a hardened realist and I believe (and continue to experience in my own life), that when you know what you want it will be easier to find a direction to go in. You will establish your own values for items and time. Desires must get written down and detailed out into working plans. That doesn't mean that everything will happen as planned or hoped. *But when you don't know what you want you are susceptible to accept anything that comes your way.*

Wealth & Assumptions worksheet:

Do you think there is a difference between high income and wealth? If so, what is it?_____

Do you have assumptions about wealth? What are they?_____

Do you have an honest assessment of how much you can feasibly and probably earn? How much is that?_____

Have you listed what you want and don't want from having money?_____

Do you think that your peers and who you identify with influence your spending decisions and feelings toward money?_____

Do you feel the need to show off your earning and spending capacity with high-status items? If so, why?_____

Are you willing to wait until you have the money readily available before you buy high-status items?_____

Chapter #3

Will a budget make you wealthy?

*"People will admit to almost anything except to how much money
they spend, because they don't know the answer."*

Your paycheck doesn't come with instructions on how to use it
or what to spend your money on. A budget is your self-created
instruction sheet. It will guide you towards the best use of your
money, fulfilling financial obligations and keep you from living
broke—maybe. Your budget needs to consist of sensible
purchases, living obligations (food, clothes, housing) and savings.
If your budget categories include: Recreational drugs, excessive
drinking, irresponsible spending and unbridled gambling you're
still going to go broke no matter how closely you stick to *that*
budget.

A budget may not *make* you wealthy but it will help keep you
from living broke. A budget will not increase your pay but it can
help you earn more money and it will help you better use, retain
and save more of the money you do earn. A budget doesn't control
what's coming in, it helps you control what's ***going out***, and that's
your defensive play against living broke.

You don't have to live by a budget, even though you probably
already do in some manner. You know that you HAVE to pay your
rent or you'll be evicted. You know that you have to pay for food,
unless you're stealing it. You know that there are certain bills you
MUST pay. Those bills usually get paid first and then whatever's
left over from your paycheck gets spent on... um, who knows
what? That may not be a formal or very good budget, but if you're
responsible enough to know that you have to pay rent and utilities
first—you're living on a budget.

All of the successful and financially self-sufficient people I know of live according to some sort of printed or written out budget, even those who have plenty of money. Any of the successful and profitable businesses I know of operate through budgets. Apparently the principle of budgeting helps toward wealth accumulation and wealth maintenance for companies and individuals. Even our government (Federal, State and Local) operate on budgets. However, we're all well aware of how a budget doesn't work if you don't stick to it, it's ridiculous or you don't have the income to support it.

Some budgets are highly detailed and use complicated mathematical equations. Most personal and family budgets use basic mathematics. Now, if all you want to do is buy more stuff and live your life showing off all of your high-status material items then there is a real simple, singular mathematical equation: **You have to earn more money if you want to be able to spend more money.** But let me repeat that earning more money, then spending most or all of it doesn't and won't make you wealthy. You can be a high-earner and still be living paycheck-to-paycheck wondering if you'll be able to pay all of your bills. Budgeting helps you make your money do more things for you.

Have you ever asked yourself, "Where did all my money go?" If you had established and lived by a budget you would know the answer, and if you didn't like the answer you would know what expenses you need or want to pare down or eliminate. Budgets help YOU control what is YOURS. It gives you a point of reference and a defense against impulsive or unnecessary spending. But YOU still have to exhibit self-control and stay within the parameters of your budget.

Are you surprised when your auto insurance premium is due? Why? You knew it was coming due, you knew you would have to pay it. I laugh at how people act "surprised" when regular bills show up. Were you hoping that the electric company would just forget about you and stop sending you bills? Are you unpleasantly surprised when your credit card statement arrives? You double check all the numbers to make sure it adds up correctly (I've done this.). "How did I spend so much?" you ask. Living with and within a budget helps get rid of surprises like that.

A budget doesn't give you more money to spend; it helps you spend what money you have more wisely. And a budget doesn't change your financial situation—right now—if you're heavily in debt, or earn less than your current obligations. But a budget can give you hope for the future and it can help you find a level of financial stability. So even if your current situation looks bleak or you're heavily in debt, a budget **will** help give you direction, help you dig yourself out of debt, put you in better control of your money and get more utility out of your money—providing that you stick to your budget.

Your "spending budget" will be limited to how much your current net income is. You can't have a $30,000 budget if you only make $20,000. Yes, you will have spending limits but at least you'll know where your money is going and have a better grasp on deciding where it should go, what to buy and where you can pare unnecessary and useless expenses. If you've been living your life randomly spending all of your money between paychecks, then setting up a budget—that consumes all of your money—with spending direction and category spending limits, won't feel that unusual. The biggest difference will be that you'll find yourself paying attention to what you buy, feeling good about yourself and more than likely living better. A budget will be easier to follow than you might think.

You can still have high-status flashy things as part of your budget. Budgeting doesn't mean you only eat gruel, keep the heat at 60 degrees in the winter and never use your air conditioner in the summer. Budgeting doesn't mean you torture yourself and live like a pauper. Budgeting means you know how much money you're spending and what you're spending it on. This simply helps you make wiser buying decisions and get the most utility possible out your money.

Budgeting is the act of you tracking your *fixed* monthly expenses, like rent, car payments, insurance, cable, phone, internet, etc., along with other *non-fixed* expenses like food, entertainment, vacations, etc., and then balancing that figure against your monthly income, comparing to make sure you have enough income to cover all of those expenses. The monthly amounts you establish for your budget are equated by tracking the annual totals you spend on things. Fixed expenses like rent or car payments are fairly easy to total up. Those MUST be paid. Whatever is left over will go towards your other non-fixed categories. Non-fixed expenses will become fixed amounts when you establish your budget categories.

For instance, you may pay your auto insurance quarterly but the cost is based on the annual premium. If your auto insurance is $600 a year your quarterly payments are $150. Within your budget you would allocate $50 of your monthly pay to go towards your auto insurance category. (If you get paid every two weeks then $25 of your check goes towards insurance.) You will hold that money in your checking account until the quarterly payment is due. Some months it will *look* like you have more money than you need in your checking account. Don't randomly spend that money just because it's there. You establish your budget and sit on the funds so you're not surprised or in a cash crunch when your quarterly, semiannual and annual bills come due. You want that money available to pay those bills.

If you were once a hyper-spender, living within a budget can be a challenging if not difficult existence—at first. Why? Because if you were raised or spent most of your life (up until now), spending every penny that ever came into your hands, controlling what goes out may feel like a punishment. But it isn't a punishment. You're taking control and setting the stage for greater things to happen and YOU will be the designer and creator of those things. With time and practice, living with and within a budget becomes easier. As you see and experience the benefits of budgeting you will feel better about your decision and about yourself. Budgeting and planning can actually turn into a fun way of life.

A budget is not glamorous. In fact, it may look downright ugly if your current bills or purchasing desires are higher than your income. Math is truth and the truth may not be pretty. After you work out your budget you might see that the only way you can fulfill your obligations and begin building a savings will require that you pare down or eliminate some of your frivolous desires. At that point you might just say, "Screw this!" and go back to wanton hyper-spending. That's your choice, but then you'll be living broke.

Real budgets.

I'm going to present two examples of personal budgets. The first example is my own budget which I live by. The second is an example of a budget I helped a married couple with two children come up with. Just look at these sample budgets and let them inspire you to come up with a custom budget of your own, based on your status, obligations and desires. You can use fancy "budget" software to help prompt you along, but I believe in the old fashioned way of writing it out on paper. You can get free pens at your bank and write on the back of scrap paper. (See how cheap I am? Even developing my budget costs me nothing.)

I have been living by a budget for more than 30 years. I haven't always stayed within my budget limits and when I didn't those were predictably the periods in my life when I had the most stress. I always wanted to hide from the truth (usually by getting drunk and wasting more money), but looking at my budget and looking at my actual spending helped me see where my overspending happened. I had to reel myself in and get control of my spending. Once I got back on track and stayed within budget I became calm again.

My budget will be far different from what yours will be. My marital status, obligations and desires will be different than yours. I don't have a mortgage payment because I paid my mortgage off early by following a budget. I don't have an auto payment because

I only buy vehicles that I can afford to pay for outright. I am single and I have no children. My recreation and entertainment desires are minimal. I have pretty low budget requirements at this point in my life, but my budget is fluid—I review it every 6 months and make corrections, additions, subtractions or adjustments according to changes in my life or changes in my desires.

When I was married our budget was much higher. It did include mortgage payments, auto payments, more obligations and purchasing categories, but we also had two incomes to cover our higher budget. Our budget was always fluid. As debts were paid off (auto loans, credit cards, etc.), we could reallocate those funds towards savings instead of more spending. Savings and investments have ALWAYS been a category in my budgets. If we needed to (or wanted to) buy a different car or some luxury item we would look at our budget and decide what could be pared down or where we could reallocate funds. Regardless of how young and foolish we (mostly me) were, we always had an honest grasp that our budget and spending could not exceed our income.

So with all that said, here is my budget, as set on 01/01/15, for Mark Tuschel, a single male with no children. There are main categories with subcategories. I list items and categories for anything I have with a monthly or annual financial commitment. These are my *fixed* expenses. I may pay my bills weekly, monthly, quarterly or seasonally, but I attempt to list everything I either know or presume that I'll buy. Some expenses are general (*non-fixed*) such as in the "food" category. I've established a monthly dollar amount that I feel is sufficient to feed me and I limit myself to spending that amount on food. I don't list meat, produce, dairy, etc. separately on my budget. I do prepare a grocery lists and make certain that I stay within the allotted budget amount. Some weeks more money is spent on dairy than meat, it may be reversed the next week, but I stay within budget. My budget guides me through my spending decisions.

In these example budgets you'll see that the annual figures are the middle column and the monthly obligation figures are in the far right column. I do this so I can clearly see how much I have to earn—every month—to pay my bills. I've also put a red asterisk after certain categories. These are fixed expenses, the amount owed doesn't change. A blue asterisk denotes fixed obligations but I can control (within reason) how much I spend. A is for discretionary purchases. If my income were to suddenly collapse those discretionary items would be the first to be dropped from my budget.

Single Male / Homeowner Budget

Category:	Annual cost:	Monthly cost:
Food*	$3,600.00	$300.00
Home Hygiene* (Cleaning supplies, etc.)	$240.00	$20.00
Personal Hygiene* (Soap, shampoo, dental, laundry det., etc.)	$420.00	$35.00
Personal products (clothing, home décor, etc.)	$600.00	$50.00
Gym membership	$540.00	$45.00
Gifts (B-Days, Christmas or Charities)	$900.00	$75.00
Entertainment (iTunes, books, dining out, etc.)	$1,200.00	$100.00
Dogs* (Food & Vet)	$360.00	$30.00
Homeowners Ins.*	$600.00	$50.00
Property Taxes*	$4,620.00	$385.00
Sewer & Water*	$480.00	$40.00
Gas & Elect.*	$1,680.00	$140.00
Home maint.*	$600.00	$50.00
Auto Ins.*	$300.00	$25.00
Auto fuel & maint.*	$1,200.00	$100.00
Mutual Funds/Retirement*	$3,600.00	$300.00
TOTALS	**$20,940.00**	**$1,745.00**

You'll notice that in my budget I don't have a cable TV bill, land line telephone bill, Netflix bill or any of those types of services. I don't need those things. I use my community library for books, CD and DVD rentals (it's FREE). My health insurance, cell phone and internet service are paid for by my company (which I own). Those costs still come out of my "pocket" but they are deductable expenses for my company, which also has a budget. I am fortunate to be in good health (I'm sure that exercising regularly at the gym, eating properly and living as a non-drinker has nothing to do with that), so I don't have any prescription medications I must co-pay. I am not a member of any religious organization, so there is no category for tithing or donations, but that may be a part of your budget.

I do use credit cards for many of my purchases—those purchases which are all part of my budget—and then I pay the balance monthly, that's why you don't see credit cards as part of my budget. I also round-up figures. If my annual auto insurance premium is $294.56 I round-up my monthly obligation to $25. I have very low auto insurance because I opt for the highest deductible and have a low-risk driving record. I also have all of my insurances through the same agent and same insurance company, so I receive a multiple policy discount. I have a very low demand for clothing and home décor. I'm a single male (with low to no fashion sense and I don't care about fancy clothes) and I have already acquired my suites, furniture and home décor items. I think that my food budget is fairly high but I desire to eat well. I am typically under budget in food and other discretionary categories, so I move the balances over to entertainment.

Once again I wish to point out that my Mutual Fund/Retirement contribution is a **fixed part** of my budget and always has been. The money that goes into my Mutual Funds is automatically withdrawn from my checking account on the same date every month. I will pare down or forego something else to meet that obligation. **I MUST PAY MYSELF FIRST and be responsible for the security of my own financial future**. Anything left over in my budget gets sent to my investments. If I earn above my monthly obligation, that money is also allocated to investments. I'm not simply hoarding money. If I need to replace my vehicle or want to make a large purchase I request a withdrawal/redemption from one of my Funds. My money doesn't just sit on my dresser waiting to get spent. It's held in investments—working for me— earning interest, dividends and capital appreciation until I need it or want it.

My budget gives me direction. It helps me make wiser buying decisions and I also know exactly what minimum income I need to earn annually to continue living at my current standard. Yet these figures still seem outrageous to me. I shock myself at how much I spend and how much it costs me to live—and I don't have a mortgage, auto loan, rent payment or debts.

At this stage in my life I have (what I consider to be) a very luxurious budget. Yet because I'm cheap, I still feel that it's fairly high. My food budget is high because I want to eat well and I can afford to appropriate money towards entertainment and recreation. And isn't that the point of money—to enjoy it? I have a pretty easygoing budget and I'm not even close to retirement age. This is a result of budgeting, saving, investing and living below my means (income) all of my life. I'm not bragging, I'm sharing a truth. If I can do this—a former drunk, drug addict and high school dropout—I have confidence that YOU can do this. The question is: **Will you?**

The next budget example is for Mike and Karen, a married couple with 2 children (plans are for their kids to attend public school), renters, who are saving to buy a home. Naturally they have many more categories than I do but they also have two incomes. Mike works fulltime and Karen works part-time. Most of the increase in categories and financial demands are due to the size of their family. Their 2 girls are twins (4 years old). Here is a budget I prepared for them, based on the information they were able to give me.

Married couple/2 children/Renter Budget

Category:	Annual cost:	Monthly cost:
Food	$9,600.00	$800.00
Home Hygiene (Cleaning supplies, etc.)	$480.00	$40.00
Personal Hygiene/Parents (Soap, shampoo, dental, laundry det., etc.)	$900.00	$75.00
Personal products/Parents (clothing, etc.)	$1,800.00	$150.00
Girl's personal products (Clothes, trinkets, etc.)	$2,400.00	$200.00
Girl's personal hygiene (Soaps, bath toys, etc.)	$1,200.00	$100.00
Gifts (B-Days, Christmas)	$1,800.00	$150.00
Entertainment (Cable, movies, dining out, etc.)	$3,000.00	$250.00
Dog (Food & Vet)	$240.00	$20.00
Renters Ins.	$288.00	$24.00
Rent	$9,000.00	$750.00
Cell phones	$1,080.00	$90.00
Gas & Elect.	$2,160.00	$180.00
Home decor.	$2,400.00	$200.00
Auto Ins. (Combined)	$2,640.00	$220.00
Auto #1 (payment)	$3,240.00	$270.00
Auto #2 (payment)	$2,760.00	$230.00

Auto fuel & maint (Combined)	$3,360.00	$280.00
Mutual Funds/Home savings	$2,400.00	$200.00
TOTALS	**$50,748.00**	**$4,229.00**

In Mike and Karen's budget I didn't list medical expenses, medical co-pay or medical insurance. I was led to believe that medical insurance is a benefit through Mike's employer but I can safely presume that he must pay a portion of it and I'm sure his part of the premium is deducted directly from his paycheck. There must certainly be co-pay for medications and doctor visits but those expenses aren't listed. There is no category for school supplies, books, etc., because the girls aren't in school yet, but I'm sure they buy them educational toys or materials. And when the girls do start school in the next year or two I'm certain they will need books and supplies and their clothing requirements will increase. Where will that money come from?

There is no category for daycare because Mike and Karen have not and do not have to pay any because each of their parents take turns watching the girls during the day (for now). What if Mike and Karen move their family to a different city or the parents move or are no longer able to watch the girls? That free daycare will come to an end. And if Mike and Karen do move to a different city they may not like the public school system, then what? How will they pay private school tuition?

Mike and Karen have not started a savings or investment account for their children's education as of yet but that absolutely should be part of their budget. I don't foresee them starting a tuition fund for their girls anytime soon. They are currently in the "home savings" mode. However, once they do buy a home their budget will increase due to mortgage, homeowners insurance, maintenance, décor, landscaping, grills, you name it. I imagine at that point they will no longer be "saving" any money for their future. I'm confident we could find a few more categories I missed that should be added to this budget as well, which would increase it considerably.

Mike and Karen were in total shock when I showed them this budget. "There's no way we spend that much money. That's about exactly how much we make." All I could say was, "Well apparently you DO spend that much money because if you didn't you would have more in savings." As it turns out they don't have anything set aside in a home savings account or any savings account for that matter. (They expect Grandpa to give them the down payment money when they find the right house—that's if they even qualify for a mortgage.)

In this budget they have no vacation category, yet they told me they take the kids on vacations with their parents. Where does the money come from for that? Mom and dad, grandma and grandpa? Credit cards? But there is no category for credit cards at all. I can't imagine that Mike and Karen don't have credit cards or don't carry any credit card debt.

This is a budget I prepared based on expenses they could *remember*. Some expenses are fact; such as rent, car payments, cell phone, etc. But most were based on, "I think we pay this much..." So I wasn't working with exact amounts. I know that these figures and this budget terrified them. "I don't think this is realistic Mark. There's no way we can come up with that kind of money." But they already do come up with that kind of money, they just don't know what they're spending it on. And what's their alternative? To keep hiding from the truth?

It's easier to hide from reality and continue living in financial **Make-believe Land**, bouncing along paycheck-to-paycheck, than it is to face the harsh truth of the numbers. But the truth will eventually catch up with them and when it does it won't be very pretty. There are so many categories and discretionary expenses they could pare down to reallocate money towards their children and savings. But I highly doubt that Mike and Karen will do that or follow this budget. I can only hope that this gets them thinking and talking about ways they can conserve and get better utility out of their money and use this as groundwork to create a workable budget of their own.

At the beginning of this chapter I told you what a budget *won't* do for you. Let's go over some of the things a budget *will* do for you—providing you stick to it. A budget helps you control small impulsive purchases. As you're physically reaching for something in a store (or getting ready to click 'buy now' on a website) you should be asking yourself, "Is this part of my budget? Will this purchase help or hinder me from staying on budget?" Small, impulsive purchases add up quickly to big numbers, which is why many people are unpleasantly surprised when they open their credit card statements. Following your budget will give you direction and help you control small impulsive purchases.

A budget shows you your history and past buying patterns, giving you choice and opportunity for the future. You will discover money wasting patterns and have the choice to eliminate unnecessary expenses and pare down other expenses. In some categories you will spend more than you budgeted. This may be a result of unexpected catastrophes, changes in weather conditions or other conditions which are out of your control. That's when you reevaluate and reallocate from one category to another. Specific items are fixed costs, like rent, mortgage or auto payments. But you do have more control over discretionary costs than you think. Just because you've always spent $95 a month for Premium Cable Service doesn't mean you have to keep that amount as part of your budget expenses. Do you really watch all the Premium channels? Do you really use all of the on-demand services? Can you dump the Premium channels and get 'Basic Cable' for half what you're paying now?

Apply this same style of questioning to all discretionary budget categories. "Can I increase my deductible on insurances? Can I eliminate certain services from my internet, data or cell plan?" You might be paying monthly dues or subscriptions for services you don't even use and simply forgot to cancel. And even with services and subscriptions you're aware of, ask yourself, "Do I still buy that or need that?" Even if there's a cancelation or termination fee, that fee may be less *now* than the total amount you'll end up paying for a service you don't need, want or use. (We'll go over the concept of "earning more by spending less" in chapter #5.) Review and adjust your budget every 6 months or as life conditions change. Reevaluate and reallocate funds from one category to another. A budget does you no good if you don't stick to it and you **DO** have more control over your costs and expenses than you think.

Life is not meant to be all sacrifice and suffering. You will sacrifice at various times in your life, but you're sacrificing now so you can build financial security and enjoy future rewards, and all of those rewards aren't that far off in the future. You should indulge yourself with some type of pleasurable rewards: short-term, monthly, annual and long-term. Make little rewards part of your personal budget.

What do you think is the one thing most people hate to admit or don't want to talk about? Go ahead and think I'll give you a few seconds. Okay, times up. It seems that we'll openly admit to just about anything **except** that we're poor money managers. We would rather present an *image* of false wealth than have people think we're not rich. We would rather keep on blindly spending and charging, thinking that we'll earn enough to pay it all off someday. We would rather look around at all of our "stuff" and believe that we're wealthy than actually know what our genuine net worth is. We'll do almost anything to avoid sitting down with a pen and a pad of paper and do a realistic accounting of how much we spend and what our innumeracy costs us in terms of actual money. That's because it's personal, the numbers really hit home and they can be scary, but they don't have to be.

People will often complain that they're always broke, that they can't make ends meet, that they don't make enough money, that they don't get paid enough. Look, I've been poor and when I was I had to make ends meet. I had to accept that I must live within my means and a budget helped me do that. I still can't buy (or worse yet—charge) everything I want. I still have to pare and cut expenses and forgo some things. But knowing what I'm up against gives me a chance to plan my defense. A budget helps me defend myself from living broke.

Look, if you can afford all the costs associated with hyper-spending and living without a budget, what do I care what you do with your money. But most of us barely make enough to cover our bills and save some money for the future. But making ends meet, living within your means and saving money for your future can be done.

Sometimes the numbers look mighty ugly while working on your own budget and things may look pretty bleak. But without the truth—knowing exactly how much you spend and what you spend it on—you'll just keep digging yourself deeper into a financial hole. Eventually you'll get so deep in that hole that you can't toss the dirt out and it begins to pile up on top of you and you end up burying yourself. Your budget should be realistic to your financial condition, meaning feasible and probable. You must have a detailed plan. Without a plan you are susceptible to acting and reacting on impulses.

I know that it may seem like I'm beating this subject to death, but I want to impress upon you **how important it is to structure your life according to a budget**. If you want to get more utility out of the money you earn, have less financial stress and begin building your own wealth, then you do need some sort of budget. Cognition of how much money is *coming in* and control of how much money is *going out* is the key to getting the most utility out of your resource of money. A budget is your best defense against living broke!

Denial of facts only harms you. I'll admit that it isn't thrilling to sit and work out a budget and go over the numbers, to analyze how much is coming in versus how much you have to pay out. It isn't pleasant, so we default to denial (and credit cards). Innumeracy only bolsters denial. Innumeracy is a lack in the acceptance and understanding of basic mathematical truths. Numbers don't lie. You may not like the results you see, but they are truth.

I'm being delusional and innumerate if I *think* I have more money than I do or I *think* that I'll earn more than I will. When I'm delusional and innumerate I won't behave according to mathematical truth. I will overspend or perceive my innumeracy as fact. For instance I can be innumerate when I consider my earnings. If I think to myself, "Let's see. I make $10.00 an hour and I work 40 hours a week, therefore I earn $400 a week and that's what I can spend." Not true. I may have *earned* $400 but then there are taxes, deductions or automatic withdrawals that I must take into account. You might be saying, "Duh, no kidding Mark. I know this." But many people honestly don't consider their actual **net pay**, even though they see it on their paystub. They just think about their wage and spend with that amount in mind. That is innumeracy.

Big problems arise when you compare your life to someone else's life. You can desire and aspire to achieve what others have, but comparing your life to someone else's will only arouse feelings of inadequacy within you and you'll likely start spending far beyond your means and your budget.

Budgeting may be old knowledge to some of you. And for those of you who are new to the concept of budgeting this may sound boring and a torturous way to live. But to the contrary—a budget can be exciting, freeing and the first step towards **you** amassing the wealth you desire.

If you don't know the actual numbers of what's coming in and what must be paid out to fulfill bills and other survival expenses (food, clothes, etc.) and accept them as truth, then you can easily end up falling prey to innumeracy, always overspending and living broke. Defend your money with a budget.

Budget Worksheet:

Can you modify the sample budget(s) I presented in this chapter and create a personalized one for yourself?_____

What do you want a budget to do for you?_____

How much time are you willing to put in to track your past expenses and create a budget?_____

Will you review your budget every 6 months, adjust and adapt it as life goes on?_____

How will you reward yourself for starting and staying on budget?_____

Have you included a savings or investment account in your budget?_____

How important is paying yourself first and will you pay yourself first? How much?_____

Looking at your past buying patterns, have you discovered expenses that you can eliminate or pare down?_____

Looking at your past purchases, have you discovered dues or subscriptions to things that you no longer use or simply forgot about? Have you canceled them?_____

Do you know people who live by a budget? How does it work for them?_____

Will you use your budget to begin building your wealth?_____

Chapter #4

A dollar is a dollar

"I really didn't lose anything, I was playing with their money."

Money doesn't have feelings. Money shows no favoritism. Money doesn't care about your race, gender, religious beliefs or political philosophy. $1 in the pocket of an African American Republican male is the same as $1 in the pocket of a White Democrat man or a Catholic Hispanic woman. There may be inequality in pay among races and genders, but that's not part of the discussion here. Money is NOT racist or sexist. One dollar is the same dollar no matter whose pocket or purse it's in. And a dollar is still a dollar no matter where or how you save it, spend it or earn it.

The actual value of $1 doesn't change regardless of where the dollar originated. True, there may be tax implications on *how* the dollar was earned or gained, but it's still a dollar. You may have earned it, found it, won it, inherited it, received it as interest or a dividend or stole it—it's still a dollar. And spending the dollar costs $1 and it consumes the same amount of time to spend it regardless of how the dollar was obtained. A dollar is still a dollar.

There are many strange interpretations and mental deceptions surrounding the value of $1 depending on where it came from. When you find money in your laundry you get excited. But found money in the laundry was always your money to begin with. It's not new money. Plenty of us misplace, lose or forget money in our clothes, car, furniture or it slips off and falls behind the dresser. It's fun to find it again. "Hey look, I found that $20 bill I thought I lost. Let's go spend it." Mentally it looks like newly found money to you. And mentally you viewed it as already gone and you made due without it, so when you do find it again you feel like you can just go frivolously spend it. But it was always your money. Why not add it to your savings when you find your own lost money? Oh, because that's not as much fun as spending it on something.

Even if you find a $20 bill on the street—it's YOUR money. I think it's interesting that people will spend "found money" far quicker and looser than money they earn at work. This is a result of mental accounting deception taking place. You might never spend $20 of your wages on lottery tickets but this was "free money." It might have been free because you found it, but if your pay rate at work is $10 an hour it would have taken you at least 2-¼ hours of your labor to earn that $20. Why not treat it the same way as if you had worked for it?

And that "found money" may cost you more than the amount you found. If you find a $20 bill and then go buy something for $30 (that you wouldn't have bought if you hadn't found this money), you are **for fact** out $30 of your own money. But you'll play a game of mental accounting deception by saying, "It only cost me $10 because I found $20." No, all of that $30 was yours and now it's gone. Inheritance money can be like this. I know people who have inherited $50,000 only to end up spending $100,000 (with their $50,000 being financed, with interest). They didn't feel like they were wasting money (even the amount they financed), because the inheritance was free money. They may very well enjoy all the toys they bought—and I hope they do—but regardless of the inheritance being free, it was their money. Mental accounting deception made them feel like they weren't spending their money, but it was theirs and now it's gone.

Sometimes it's fun to go spend found money. It's fun to take that $20 bill you found on the street and go buy something frivolous like lottery tickets or treat yourself and a friend to Starbucks. That's what money is for, to have fun with. Just be cognizant of what you're doing and don't play a game of mental accounting deception. If you want to tell yourself that found money is free money (even inheritance), and you want to spend it,

70

then spend it. But remember that regardless of how you got it, it was your money, that it's now gone and it can't be used for something else.

Here's another example of the mental accounting deception people play on themselves with their own money. Let's say you're sitting in a casino at a Blackjack table and you happen to be up by $300. The pit boss walks up to you and pleasantly says, "I'm going to take that $300 worth of chips in front of you but you can keep the $100 you started with." You're flabbergasted. You become angry, protective and say, "You're not taking those chips, those are MY chips." The pit boss calmly responds, "Well I just heard you tell your friend here that you're playing with the house's money—I'm the house and I'm taking my money."

I'm certain that you wouldn't agree with his request nor agree with his logic, but if you happen to have lost that $300 back to the house while gambling you would likely tell your friend (and yourself), "Well I was playing with *their money*, so I really didn't lose anything." This is mental accounting deceiving you. That $300 was YOUR money no matter how you want to mentally account for it. If you were suddenly called away from the Blackjack table, or had the self-control to get up and walk away, you would **for fact** be $300 ahead and it would be YOUR money. (By the way, in the example above, the pit boss knows he doesn't have to ask for the house's money back. The house knows that you'll play mental accounting gymnastics and give it all—and more—back to them.)

This same mental accounting deception occurs with *saving money* off purchases. It seems that many people are influenced by percentages, regardless of whether it's a percentage of return on an investment, percentage off the MSRP or discount percentage on a *perceived* sale. A lot of people will drive thirty miles and use up one hour of their time to save $20 off the price of a product that was originally selling for $40. That's a 50% savings—wow, who wouldn't want to save 50%? But that same person probably won't drive the same distance and use up the same one hour to save $20 (or more) off the purchase of a product that has a cost of $500. Why? Because they perceive the percentage of savings as lower ($20 off of a $500 price tag is a mere 4% savings), however, it's still $20 and it's still one hour of their time.

Don't be fooled or influenced by percentages. Percentages are simply a mathematical equation and reference point. Focusing strictly on percentages can cloud your thinking and influence you towards making poor decisions with your money. What's more important is the bottom line; "How much **real** money are we talking about here?" Which of these sounds better to you, a 50% return or a 10% return on an investment? Naturally the 50% return sounds better, but would you rather have a 50% return on a $1,000 investment or only a 10% return on a $20,000 investment?

If you haven't figured it out yet, the 50% return earns you $500 but the 10% return earns you $2,000. The **real** dollar amount of the lower percentage is **4 times greater** than the higher percentage. I would rather have the lower percentage and the larger amount in real earnings. Don't be distracted or enamored by percentages. Percentages are simply a mathematical equation and reference points for you to use. Percentages aren't money—only money is money.

Here's where you say, "What do you mean that percentages don't matter? My credit card has 28% interest rate and I'm getting clobbered with **real** payments." Well then I would say that's a bad equation for you. Regardless if it's 12%, 28%, 36% or 78% interest, it's still just a reference point of what you'll be gouged if you carry a balance. The fact is that 12%, 28%, 36% or 78% of a zero balance is zero. As long as you don't carry a balance the interest percentage rate doesn't matter. **Carrying a balance on your credit card is the bad part of the equation**.

So yes, percentages DO matter and do make a difference. Naturally you want a higher percentage on your returns and a lower percentage levied against what you owe. But a percentage figure is still just part of an equation, allowing you to compute mathematical outcomes. Again, what matters are the hard, factual **real** dollar amounts. True, a .25% variation—up or down—on a $150,000 mortgage won't make a huge difference on your monthly payment, but it will over the life of a 30 year mortgage. The math equation of the percentage reveals the real amounts of what additional must be paid or what the payments will be reduced by. Use percentages to equate the math and make better decisions, but don't be unnecessarily enamored or influenced by the percentage number alone. Regardless of whether $1 is 50% off something or .005% off something, $1 is still $1.

More mental gymnastics.

All of the various "Everything's $1" stores know how to profit from your mental accounting gymnastics. Nothing against these stores, you can find some awesome bargains there. But I watch as people (myself included), walk through the aisles and grab items that they either don't need or normally wouldn't buy. Mentally you think, "Oh hell, it's only a dollar." By the time you get to the checkout you have $28 worth of "Oh hell, it's only a dollar," when all you really needed or wanted was $12 worth of items.

Just because something is only $1 doesn't mean it's a bargain price. For example, there are name brand bags of snacks for $1 at the $1 Store. I noticed that the bag contains 2.3oz of product. I was curious (and I'm cheap), so I walked across the street to the grocery store and noted that a big bag of the same name brand snack is $3.69 but there are 16oz in the big bag. I get almost double the product for half the price at the grocery store. (I would have to buy 7 bags at the $1 Store to get the same amount of product.) And a lot of times the grocery store will have the big bag sale priced for less than MSRP or on sale 2-for-1.

Here's another example. A 2-Pack of Scrub Sponges for washing dishes is only $1. But I know that I can buy a 12-Pack of the same sponges for $4.95 at a warehouse store like Sam's Club or Costco. (They're .50 cents apiece at the $1 Store versus .42

cents apiece at Sam's.) That's not a huge difference but every penny counts when you want to get the most distance and utility from your pennies. Also, the sponges won't rot so I won't waste money, but I do have to lay out $3.95 more *now* to buy the discount.

The $1 Store isn't a criminal for selling you snacks at twice the price or charging more per sponge, they're just taking advantage of consumer's mental accounting tricks, their innumeracy and their tendency to impulse buy. But who knows, maybe all you wanted (or should be eating) was 2.3oz of a snack. And maybe $3.69 for snacks or $4.95 for sponges doesn't fall into your budget, but $1 does. I'm not telling you that you shouldn't shop at the $1 Store; I'm simply pointing out the math. But remember that just because something is "only $1" doesn't mean it's a bargain, it just means it costs $1.

The deception of the *sale*.

"50% OFF! 2-for-1. Buy one get the second for 50% off." Retailers and advertisers use all of these tactics to get you to talk yourself into gladly buying what they want you to buy. This isn't shifty or underhanded. No one forces you to buy Fritos when they're on sale 2-for-1. You may not even really like Fritos or they aren't on your grocery list or part of your food budget, "but at 2-for-1 who can pass?" Now if you do happen to like Fritos and they are part of your snack budget, then this IS a great deal for you. Then you might want to consider stocking up, buying 10 bags for the price of 5. (They last for about 6 years if you don't open the bag, 3 years if you do.)

The U.S. government has compiled some interesting statistics on "sale item" grocery store purchases. It's no surprise that when an item goes "*on sale*" it moves off the shelves quicker and in greater volume. However, most "*sale*" items are for what many would consider as junk food or unhealthy foods. No insult intended to Frito-Lay in my junk food reference or example above, they make fine snacks, but there is something to be expanded upon here. Sale items are on sale because the store wants to sell more of those particular items. Why? Because those items hold a higher profit margin for all parties involved and those items are not as large a part of someone's normal grocery budget or spending habit. Put the item "*on sale*" and you as a consumer must either buy fewer apples (lower profit margin) to stay within spending budget, or you end up spending more than you budgeted or planned.

Produce, fruits, vegetables, organic items and the like rarely go on sale, unless it's a result of seasonal or regional abundance. Various seafood also goes "on sale" due to the same seasonal or regional abundance factors. Sales on meat are typically a result of planned bulk purchases by the grocery store. Like any smart retailer, sale items and loss-leaders are promoted primarily to get you into the store. Once you're in the store the retailer hopes to sway you into buying items that you didn't intend on buying or spend more than you had planned on spending. This tactic isn't evil or underhanded on the part of retailers, it's smart business. It's up to YOU to make the most out of these sales and discounts and have them work to your financial advantage.

This is why it's so important for you to have a food budget and make grocery lists, so you're not influenced by *sales* items. If an item you normally buy, that's part of your food budget, goes on sale you will want to stock up on it, providing it won't rot before you can consume it, thus wasting money. Then, to stay on budget, you forego purchasing something else so you don't go over budget. The next time you go shopping (according to budget), you won't have to buy Fritos—because you already have 10 bags at home— and you can buy other budget category items that you had forgone the last time you shopped or other budget items that are now on sale.

Does this all sound like a lot of work and tedious mental processing? Sure. But the end result is for you to get the most distance, product and utility out of every dollar you spend. It doesn't take a lot of work to be poor and broke, but it does require work and self-control to get the most out of your limited resource of money. Wealthy people don't become wealthy by spending foolishly and with no control.

Mortgage or rent is the highest monthly expense most people have. Groceries are typically the second highest monthly expenditure for adults. The cost of mortgage payments or rent, once the contract or lease has been signed, is typically a fixed amount, but what you spend on food is within your control. You might like and want a Ribeye steak but all you can afford within your budget is ground turkey. The decision of which to buy is within your control. You might not be very happy that you have only a limited amount of money that you can spend on food and you can't afford Ribeye steak, but that's why you really **need** to have a budget, to make lists and make wiser purchases. Sticking to your budget will keep you from living broke and using your money more wisely may let you afford Ribeye steak once in a while (but only if it's on sale).

This next part should be able to go without being said, but I feel I should mention it because some people don't think about this or take action on this. **Use coupons and sign up for grocery store discount cards**. Grocery stores have a variety of promotions where you build points with purchases and those points can be applied towards some other promotion or purchase. I shop at one grocery store chain in particular because my purchases accrue towards discount credits at participating gas stations. I accrue .05 cent per gallon gas credit for every $50 I spend. Eventually I build up enough points and I get a .50 cent per gallon discount on gas. I'm limited to 20 gallons with the discount but that comes to $10. I have to buy both food and gas, so I try to get the most utility with my food money purchases. I'll even let people use my store discount card. They get the card discounts and I build more points. I've gotten more than $1 per gallon off gas by doing this.

Does your grocery store have a certain day during the week where you get "Double Coupons?" That means if you have a coupon for .50 cents off a product they will match it and you get

$1 off. That day may not fall into your schedule or it's inconvenient for you, so what? You can truly save (and get more utility out of) a lot of money that you have to spend on food anyway if you shop on those days. Watch for these kinds of promotions, buy items that are on sale and sign up for store discount cards. Compare discount card promotions between grocery store chains. Go with the promotion that best suits your needs. Use coupons and discounts. Why would anyone want to pay more for something than they have to? It's your responsibility to yourself to make sure that you get every penny of value out of your food money.

Believe me, wealthy people use coupons and hunt for food discounts all the time. They might want Ribeye steak today but if some other meat is on sale they'll buy that instead. They know that eventually Ribeye steak will be on sale, and when it is on sale they'll buy it then. Wealthy people are not too proud or embarrassed to use coupons and store discount cards, they don't need to impress the cashier by paying full price for everything. You don't become wealthy by spending more, you build and retain wealth by spending less.

Businesses are in business to make money.

The goal of any good business is to make it as easy as possible to separate you from your money. If a business isn't doing that then they're not a very good business and won't be in business for very long (and I won't invest in them). This doesn't mean that businesses are evil or underhanded. Just like you as an employee, don't you want your employer to pay you the highest wage, or at the very least, a fair wage for your labor? Does that make you evil? (I don't think I've ever heard anyone say, "Boss, you're paying me too much. Please reduce my pay by $1 an hour.") A good business wants to earn a fair profit by selling you a decent product or service that you will be happy with. Their mission is to make it as enticing and as easy as possible for you to buy their product or service. Even non-profits and benevolent organizations want to make it as enticing and as easy as possible for you to donate your money.

But just because a business wants you to get value and be happy with their product or service, that doesn't mean they always have your best interest in mind. "0% Financing to qualified credit. No payments for 6 months. Cancel at any time." These promotions are all intended to incentivize you to part with your money, or more money than you have, when you had no intention of doing so. Yet many of these promotions can be used in your best financial interest—providing it's a promotion that happens at the same time you were planning on making a purchase.

I've had the good fortune to encounter promotions when I was already in the midst of shopping for a product. The promotion actually worked in my interest and the store earned my business just for incentivizing others to spend money they didn't have. For example, I needed and then bought a floor model washing machine from a national hardware store. Just for using their store credit card I had the choice of either no payments for 6 months or a 2% in-store rebate. I was planning on paying for the washer in full so I opted for the 2% in-store rebate of $14. That might not sound like a lot of money, but I didn't build any new debt and I didn't carry any debt on the card, plus I had $14 that I could spend towards something else I would eventually need from that hardware store. This is just one example. I always look for and weigh out the various promotions when I'm shopping for something that costs $100 or more.

You don't have to just hope you'll get lucky and see a promotion when you need something. Somebody somewhere will be running some kind of special on the product you need. Search the newspaper ads, watch for the ads on TV or search different store's websites. Most national chains have "price matching" policies (even grocery stores). Take the competitor ad in with you. Don't be embarrassed to do this. Who are you trying to impress by paying full price if you don't have to? The cashier? This is YOUR money at stake here. Your loyalty is to your own wallet, not to a certain brand or store.

Look closely at credit card and store credit card offers. **"5% cash back on all purchases!"** That looks tempting, but did you read the rules and restrictions? With a lot of them you receive your "cash back" only once a year and the "cash back" check can only be cashed, or is only valid for purchases at their store. That's okay if you shop there regularly, but they're still holding **your** "cash back" money for a year. Oh, and if you miss a payment or are late on a payment you lose all of your credits and won't be earning any new credits until your account is back in "good standing." And what does "good standing" mean? Does it mean my current balance has to be paid in full along with all future balances being paid in full before cash back begins accruing again? Credit card companies know that the majority of people incentivized by these kinds of offers will at some point forget to make a payment, make only the minimum payment or somehow fall out of "good standing" and thus lose all of their cash back credits.

A few credit card companies allow you to apply your credits monthly towards your bill or outstanding balance (very few). Some will even send you a check or make a deposit into your bank account (even fewer). This is a nice gesture and a highly customer oriented feature offered by the credit card company. But most credit card companies will "incentivize" you to use your points towards more purchases at a participating retailer instead of taking the credit or cash back. Making more purchases is what most people do with their points because it's "free money."

Have you ever used credit card points for an airline ticket? If you have I'm sure you spent money or charged something before and after you got off the plane. Maybe you even took the trip or went on a vacation because you didn't want your points to expire. I'm not criticizing or advocating against using credit card point "incentives" towards airline tickets. I'm just stating the true purpose behind the promotions—the credit card companies want you to spend more, charge more, carry a balance and then charge you interest to earn a profit.

Then there's "Double points and added points" for buying specific products like gas or shopping at specific stores during a limited time. These can be fantastic promotions for you to take advantage of. But the credit card companies know that a greater majority of people will buy more than they had planned and then carry the balance. The credit card company knows that they'll earn more in interest from the people who carry a balance than what they have to pay out in cash, credits or airline tickets to people like me and you. When I see a genuine "Double Points, Bonus Points or Cash back" offer from a credit card company, that's the card I use, as long as it's for my budget items. Then I pay the balance in full and I apply the credit towards my next payment or request a check if either of those are allowed.

Take advantage of credit card promotional offers, but make sure that it's an offer you'll use or will be of benefit to you. If you're planning a vacation, then ramp up those airline ticket points and read the terms closely to see if or when those points might expire. The rules and restrictions of promotions might be in very teeny-tiny type, but they're right there on the back of your statement and on their website. Pay off your balance monthly, use points promotions for YOUR benefit and become one of the small percentages of people who actually profit off the credit card companies.

Why do you think manufacturers offer rebates? To get you to look at the math—as they want you to see it—and get you to buy their product NOW. Believe me, they're not interested in saving you money, they're interested in moving boxes. The company is not evil, they're in business to sell products and make money. You absolutely can benefit from these rebate offers, but don't be fooled by their math.

Sample rebate:

$100 Regular price
-$50 Rebate
This great thing is **ONLY $50**

    Well it really isn't $50 and here's why. You have to pay sales tax (which could be up to 10%) on the $100 that the item costs now *before rebate*. So you're laying out $100+ tax **right now**. Then you have to actually send in the required rebate materials. (The majority of people who make a "rebate incentivized" purchase never do this step.) Then you will wait 6-8 weeks to receive your rebate check. Is it a real check or an in-store credit? If it's an in-store credit for $50 you still have to pay sales tax on the $50 purchase when you use the credit to buy something from their store. If it's a real check you can cash it or deposit it into your own bank account without paying income or sales tax. The latter are the rebates I like where I receive a real check.

    There are reasons why retailers and manufacturers like to promote a rebate instead of simply putting the item "on sale." Primarily it's because the majority of buyers won't do the work to get the rebate redemption. Paying full price now and waiting for a rebate also has to do with "gross revenue" and accounting window-dressing strategies companies use, but that isn't worth discussing here. State Revenue Departments prefer rebates as well. Why? Because they get to collect the full sales tax on the price *before* the rebate. If the product is $100 with a 6% sales tax, the store collects $106. The State gets $6 and you eventually get the $50 rebate making your final cost $56. If the rebate is an in-store credit of $50, and you use the in-store credit to buy something, you pay $3 in sales tax, making your final cost $59 on the original product. The State ultimately receives a total of $9 on this series of transactions. Now if the product was simply put "on sale" for $50 with a 6% sales tax, your final cost would be $53. You would spend $3 less and the State would receive only $3 in total tax revenue instead of $9. Hmmm, who's evil here?

I am not saying that every rebate, sales promotion, credit card promotion or store card promotion is a con job or a scam solely designed to separate you from your money. Stores do put items on sale (sometimes called loss-leaders), to entice you into their store. Grocery stores do this all the time. Once you're in the store the retailer hopes you'll grab at a few more items that you hadn't intended on buying or something else that might be discounted. A manufacturer or producer may want to move a product fast for their own internal business reasons and they will then reduce the cost to the store. Sales and rebates are a great way to "earn more by spending less," and get the most utility out of your money—providing that it's a product you use or had already intended to buy, within your budget.

Rebate offers are often incentives for you to forego your brand loyalty and try out a different manufacturer. A certain rebate may tilt you from buying manufacturer 'A' towards buying manufacturer 'B'. In many cases and with many products there isn't much difference in quality or warranty between name brands. That's when a rebate or sale might sway you to try LG instead of Sony.

But mostly, rebates are really intended to get you to impulsively buy a product you didn't need or never had plans on buying— made even more profitable by the high odds that you will never go through the steps to redeem the rebate. Make rebates and in-store credits work in your favor. Be mindful of what the "rules" are for the particular rebate. Be aware that you are laying out the full price right now. And absolutely go through the steps to receive your rebate—become one of the small percentages of people who profit from rebates.

Summary: How do you become a millionaire? By accumulating one million dollars, $1 at a time (actually, one penny at a time). The pennies and dollars may come rolling your way in larger chunks at times, but you still need to accumulate one million $1 bills to become a millionaire. You do this by spending fewer $1 bills than the amount of $1 bills that are coming in. The

$1,000,000 might be *held* in various asset types like stocks, real-estate, bonds or business ownership, but it will still take one million $1 bills to get there.

Many people mentally rearrange the value of a dollar (or any amount of money for that matter), depending on how they acquired the dollar, what they're spending it on or the percentage ratio the dollar falls within the equation. These are all valuation tricks and mental accounting deceptions that we play on ourselves. These mental tricks become more and more dangerous, and costly, when they are played with hundreds, thousands and tens of thousands of dollars. The face value of a dollar will always remain the same—its purchasing power will devalue over time due to inflation and a dollar's buying power will fluctuate between product types—but $1 is and will always be $1. Do what you want with your money, but at least be aware of the fact that a dollar still holds the value of one dollar no matter how you got it, spent it or saved it.

The $1 Worksheet:

How do you feel when you find money?_____

Do you save or spend found money?_____

Is $1 worth less if you found it than if you worked for it or earned it? Why?_____

Do you think inheritance is found money? How would you treat it?_____

Do you think you play mental accounting deception games with yourself?_____

Can you think of any times when you did play mental accounting games?_____

Are you more influenced by percentages than by the real dollar amount?_____

Do you look at real dollar amounts or just at percentages?_____

Do you buy products because they offer a rebate? Do you send in for the rebate?_____

Do you take full advantage of coupons and store cards?_____

Do you take full advantage of credit card promotions or do you just feed their profits by paying interest?_____

What will you do to get more distance and utility out of your money?_____

What do you think $1 is?_____

Chapter #5

Earn more by spending less

"Render unto Caesar what is Caesar's—but not a penny more."

The common line of thinking is: "If I earn more money I'll be richer and happier." The first part of that is true. If you earn more money you will have more money available to spend, but more money may get you further into debt and you may end up trying to buy your happiness purchasing the wrong *things* simply because you have more money at your disposal.

Some of material in this chapter was just covered in the previous chapter; use coupons, use store discount cards, pay credit card balances monthly—so that you get more utility out of your money and spend less of it than you need to. I have two purposes to this chapter: Purpose #1, I want to relay ideas and ways for you to *technically* increase your income by spending less, thus building your wealth. Purpose #2, I want to point out how tempting it is to spend more as your income increases, as you reduce debt and your wealth builds. (I have personal experience with both of these.) Just because you earn more and watch as your nest egg grows doesn't mean you should feel obligated to spend more. You don't just want to build wealth, you want to preserve wealth. You do this by always living *below* your income.

I fully support rewarding yourself and enjoying your money. More income means you can buy more products and do more things, but that doesn't guarantee that you will enjoy your money any more. In fact, as your income increases, living up to or a little beyond your increasing income can get you into deeper trouble. That's why I want to begin with topic #2—the temptations to spend more as you earn more. So let me tell you a story about Barry.

Barry isn't dumb. He actually thinks through his financial and personal decisions. He considers his choices and purchases. Barry doesn't earn a high income, but he does use his income wisely and lives well within his means. He's fairly conservative with his spending and he even has a savings account. He's been working at the same small manufacturing company for over 3 years. He earns $12 an hour and through budgeting (tracking past expenses and fixed expenses against his income), he has figured out how to get the most utility out of what he earns.

Barry knows he has financial constraints. Of course Barry would like to earn more so that he would have more discretionary money to spend, but he isn't unhappy with his life. He knows he needs to exhibit self-control with his money and he doesn't get impulsively carried away buying all sorts of stuff on his credit cards. He has little to no debt. He still has fun with his money; he goes on dates and takes an annual camping vacation. He budgets his earnings using simple software. He lives within his means and he always saves a fixed amount ($100 per month) of his paycheck into a savings account, then at the end of the year he moves his savings into a Roth IRA. He doesn't contribute to a 401(K) because the company he works for doesn't offer 401(K) matching. Sounds like things are pretty good for Barry so far doesn't it? Well things are about to get even better.

Barry hears that a larger company has expanded a manufacturing department and they're hiring, paying $18 an hour. He thinks this all out. He knows the other company is stable, reputable and has been in business for over 20 years. It's basically the same position, same benefits (vacation, health insurance, etc.), same hours and it's actually a mile closer to his apartment. This company also offers their employees a 401(K) program with 50% employer matching. Barry decides to apply for the job and as luck has it he gets hired. Barry's a responsible guy so he tells his present employer, works his last two weeks and leaves on good terms.

Barry just got himself a 50% pay raise. He's earning $960 per month more (his take-home pay is $700 more after taxes). He immediately signs up for the 401(K) plan and has 4% of his pre-tax income automatically deducted from his check, with his employer matching 50% of what he puts into the plan. ($172.80 per month is going into his 401(K) so he discontinues his monthly automatic savings account deposit.) Even with that 401(K) deduction Barry still has $700 per month MORE than he was used to living on. Barry has been living on a budget based on his lower income, so for the first 2 months he puts that extra money into his savings account. Smart guy that Barry.

But Barry grows accustomed to having this extra money, (it's amazing how quickly humans adapt to their conditions). Barry works out a new budget based on his new income. He can go on more dates and plans for a more luxurious vacation. He can also easily afford to get the latest iPhone and pay the monthly service fee, committing to a 2-year contract. That fancy new phone can support some cool games and apps, so he signs up for them as well—that's an extra $12 per month. Why not sign up for Netflix too? It's no big deal, he has the income to pay for it. Even after all this recent spending and added monthly commitments he still has about $350 per month more than he's been used to.

With $350 a month more Barry can get a new car. If he trades in his old car and pays a $2,000 deposit he can lease a brand new car for $295.00 per month for 3 years. He's still within his income so he takes the plunge, trades in his car and dips into his savings to pay the deposit. But the new car insurance costs more (this adds an additional $14 per month) and you certainly don't want that new car just collecting dust in the driveway so he goes more places. More gas, more entertainment expenses, more dates, more more more of everything.

All of these little additions and service fees begin adding up. $12 here, $9.95 there, dates, movies, a bit more on entertainment. None of this is a problem because Barry can afford it, but he's getting to the limit of his income. As I mentioned, what he was having automatically deducted from his paycheck and going into a savings account isn't going there anymore, instead he is contributing into a 401(K) plan. Yes, he's building wealth with that plan but he has very little choice on how that money is invested and he can't access that money until he's 59-½. He has the *right* to access that money, but there would be huge penalties and taxes for doing that, so technically that money doesn't even exist. When his money was going into a savings account he had full control and discretion on how it would be invested or spent. He had already paid taxes on that money so it was HIS money to use at any time. Anyway, back to the story.

Barry likes having more money and he enjoys spending it on cool stuff. He grows accustomed to this lifestyle. He even figures that he can spend a little more because he'll probably get a small raise when his annual review comes around. He's been at this company for 8 months and he does a good job. He's never late, insubordinate or problematic. His supervisor likes him and suggested that he apply for the position of shift leader within the department expansion he was hired for. If Barry gets that job this of course would mean even more money coming his way.

Barry has made what he believes to be some wise moves and things are going pretty darn good in his life. But Barry is unaware of some other events taking place behind the scenes at his company. The sales staff hasn't been able to secure the extension on a contract—that was the contract which sparked them to expand a department and bring on more employees. The sales staff also hasn't had much success at landing any *new* contracts because of a slowdown in their industry. These are all factors which are completely out of Barry's control and he has no knowledge of. The company and his department just keep chugging along.

But one Monday morning the news hits; indefinite layoffs for anyone with less than 2 years seniority. Barry's only been there for 9 months so he's included in these layoffs. By the end of the week Barry finds himself unemployed, strapped with debt, his savings account mildly depleted (he needed money as part of the security payment for his car lease), and facing all of his monthly contract commitments. Well this sure sucks.

Everything fell apart and Barry feels like a real dope, "Why didn't I see this coming?" But Barry's not dumb and he can't be expected to follow the fluctuations of the world economy let alone know what's going on in the back offices of his employer—he has a job to do. All that Barry should have expect of himself was to live *well below* his income, save for the future and build a financial safety net in the event some unforeseen bad luck came his way—which just happened.

Barry made some pretty good and some pretty bad decisions based on the knowledge that he had at the time. Going for a 50% pay increase was a smart move. Contributing some pre-tax earnings into a 401(K) with 50% employer match was also a smart move. Not continuing his automatic deduction into a savings account *wasn't* smart. Had he continued that savings deduction he would have grown accustomed to taking home $600 per month more instead of $700 more. He would have been living *below* his means and he would have been building his own discretionary savings account—money he could access at any time without penalty or taxes.

Buying a new iPhone and getting a new car wasn't all that dumb, at the time he had the income to pay for it. Readjusting his budget upward and spending more on entertainment wasn't all that dumb either. Barry had the income at the time but now he's faced with problems—he has a lot of bills to pay. Sure, he'll be receiving unemployment benefits but that won't start rolling in for a few weeks and those benefits will be less than half of what he was taking home. His biggest problem at the moment is that some of his bills are due NOW. What's he to do?

He goes back to his former employer but his old position has already been filled and they aren't hiring at this time (industry slowdown ya know). Barry's in a jam so he uses what's left of his savings account to cover his rent, make a lease payment and pay a couple of other monthly bills. Prior to being laid off he had ramped up the balance on his credit card a bit and now he can only afford to make the minimum monthly payment (here comes the compounding interest). He's spending a lot less on gas because he's not driving as much but his lease payments and auto insurance payments are still the same amount. His rent and other fixed expenses are still the same amount. Barry is not in a good spot right now—he owes a lot of money and has high monthly bills—but his income is far below what he needs to cover those bills. He can pare down some of his discretionary spending—buy cheaper or less food, eliminate entertainment from his life and begin canceling some of his services (oh, but there will be an early termination fee on some of those services), but he needs money NOW.

It's been a couple of months and Barry's unemployment benefits will be ending within a few months and if he doesn't find a job that pays the same $18 an hour he's screwed—he won't have the money to pay all of his current commitments. He's getting a bit nervous. He's really thinking through all of his options. His nervousness turns into fear and he starts considering some really bad options. He could take a withdrawal from his 401(K) or IRA, but that will cost him a lot of money in early withdrawal penalties, taxes and decimate his retirement savings. He can turn the leased car back in, cancel his cell phone, cancel Netflix and drastically pare down expenses. But as I just mentioned, some of these services have early termination fees. If he turns in his leased car he won't have transportation to search for a job or get to his new job when he finally does land one. It doesn't look like Barry's story is going to have a happy ending.

So how does Barry's story end? Well it continues to change. Barry does land another job, but that position pays less than the $12 an hour job he left in the beginning of this story. He pared down his expenses and a friend moved in with him so they split the rent and utility bills. He wiped out his savings account but at least he left his IRA intact. (He was also wise enough to have his 401(K) transferred over to his IRA. We'll go over that subject in chapter #11.) Barry is a smart guy and a hard worker. He will take action to help his luck and his condition move in a more positive direction. Barry will likely recover from this run of bad luck and will learn a lot from this. "Living broke sucks and I'm going to have to plan better in the future."

I'm sure many of you have been in situations similar to Barry's. The purpose of this story isn't to instill fear in you, but to illuminate that changes—changes which are completely out of your control—can and do happen. The point is to remind you that when you get a raise, advance your career, find yourself earning more or paying off a debt—meaning you have more money in your pocket—you don't have to burn through it or take on more debt. Just because you have $20 in your pocket doesn't mean you *have* to spend it. There's nothing wrong with rewarding yourself with nice things (even luxuries) when you earn more, but always live *below* your income, plan ahead and build a financial safety net for yourself. That's what genuinely wealthy people do.

How do wealthy people live?

This segment isn't just about the outward physical behaviors that you see, it's about the mental processing wealthy people perform, how and why they make financial decisions. I will be using the term "wealthy," but as I've said, wealth and the amount of money or assets a person has are subjective—wealth is different for everyone. When I say "wealthy" I'm talking about people who live comfortably but well within or *below* their income. That means they have extra money left over from every paycheck and they have a safety net saved up and have money or assets set aside for their retirement. They may or may not be "millionaires," but they're calmer knowing that they have enough money to cover their regular bills, make new purchases, have discretionary money to do some fun things and have a security net to handle unforeseen events and expenses.

Wealthy people don't necessarily get paid more than you do, but they *earn more* because they spend less. And the easiest way for you to earn more is for you to do the same. You don't have to change careers or get a raise to earn more money. By spending less of your hard earned money you will retain more of it. But there is a catch. When you spend less you have to put those "saved pennies" somewhere. Once they have accumulated into larger amounts you can then spend it on something else. (Money is worthless until it is spent or invested.) "Spending it" may mean investing it so it returns you even more money. That's what wealthy people do.

Let me give an example of how you can earn more. If you want to increase the "take home" on your paycheck by $100 you would have to earn about $140 more in gross pay because once taxes have been taken out you end up with $100 net. But if you eliminate $100 in useless or unnecessary expenditures you will have technically earned more than $240 without doing any additional work or earning any more income. How is that? Let's look at the math:

If you earn $140 gross, to net $100, and then spend it on purchases (consumables like going out to dinner, going out to bars, etc.), you have acquired no assets, have no more net worth and have net money of **zero** left. You may have had fun going out or partying, but you are left with **zero**. On the other hand, if you eliminate $100 in expenditures over the same time period—and don't spend it on something else—you will have $100 in your hands. You don't have to pay taxes on money that you didn't spend. You don't have to pay taxes on money that you didn't have to earn and you don't have to pay taxes on money that is already yours.

$140 Gross
+$100 NOT spent
=$240

You may not agree with my math or my logic and claim that you haven't earned $240, or that you haven't actually earned anything at all because no new money has come your way. But it's a might difficult to refute that if you don't spend $100, of what you already have, that you no longer have it. If you didn't spend it then it still exists and if you avoided or eliminated spending it then you are $100 ahead of where you would have been had you spent it.

Some of you might say, "Yes, but I want to earn more so I can apply it towards my 401(K) or IRA." That's wonderful, because if you do earn $140 gross, and apply it towards a tax deferred plan, you are earning and retaining the full amount—you just can't touch it yet. What I'm talking about here is having more discretionary money in your pocket NOW. What you do with that money is up to you.

By eliminating 10% of your current annual expenses you are mathematically giving yourself a 15% (or higher) annual raise. Simple math tells us that if you don't spend as much you don't have to earn as much. If you spend 10% less than you currently are, you will have 10% more cash that you can put into savings or investments.

I'm quite confident you could find areas, services and spending habits which you could save yourself 10% or more on. Invest some of your time and take a look at your current and past bills. Look for areas where you can eliminate or pare down any unnecessary or useless services or buying habits.

Here are some examples of places you can spend less: Gym memberships, club memberships, magazine and newspaper subscriptions, cable services, phone services or hobbies you no longer participate in. Can you raise your insurance deductibles? Can you eliminate or go with lower cost packages? Can you get by just fine with fewer services or limits on services? (Like basic cable, a cheaper internet service or lower data plan.) Are there services, memberships or any recurring bills for things you no longer use or forgot to cancel? If you're a smoker you could quit smoking, smoke a little less or buy a cheaper brand. If you're a drinker you could quit drinking, drink less or buy a cheaper brand.

If you have credit card balances the interest you're paying is eroding away at your future wealth. First off, check your credit card statements to see if there are any services or memberships—which you no longer need or use—that you are being automatically billed for. You might notice a .99 cent per month charge and wonder, "What is this for? Aw who cares, it's only .99 cents." Well small incidental charges add up. There is usually a phone number or company name on the same line as the charge. If not, call your credit card company and ask, "What is this for? Who is charging me? Do you have a phone number for the company?" You may have unwittingly and unknowingly agreed to some recurring fee when you "agreed" to the terms of service at a website. Look at every line item on your credit card statement.

Next, stop or control further spending on any credit card that has a balance. Do you have a card you rarely use and has no balance? Can you get a new card? Use the card with a zero balance for all current and future purchases—but for only the bare necessities—and **make sure you pay that balance off every month**. You won't pay any interest that way. Then keep paying your other cards, even if it's only the monthly minimum. You'll slowly be reducing what you owe, but more importantly you won't be increasing your balance. Credit card companies charge you on "average daily balance." This means that if you have a balance, whatever you charge *today* is added to your balance and you're paying interest on it before the billing cycle is over and before you make your next payment. You're even paying interest on your interest! This is all completely legal for them to do (it's not nice but it is legal) and you agreed to those terms when you accepted and began using the card.

Finally, consider (but only consider) consolidating credit card balances to one card. You will be charged a fee for "balance transfers," (typically 3% or 4%), but if you can go from 28% down to 13% you'll be saving yourself a lot of money on interest and paying more towards the balance. If you decide not to consolidate or can't (because you're already maxed out) then pay only the minimum on your lowest interest cards and pay as much as you can towards your highest interest cards. Another strategy is to pay off the lowest interest card first and then transfer higher interest balances to the lower interest card. Yes, this all requires math, thinking and self-control. But do you want to live broke the rest of your life? Once you have mathematical knowledge and skills you'll be able to use that knowledge and those skills to make wiser decisions in the future. Digging yourself out of debt isn't exciting but it can be rewarding and freeing as you see the end nearing.

If you can afford all of these things I just mentioned (cable, cell services, booze, smokes) or if higher insurance deductibles make you feel uncomfortable, then keep paying for all of them. But remember that every expense is an exchange. If you spend $1 towards "Service A" that means you no longer have that $1 to spend or apply towards something else.

Spending adds up over time: Wealthy people know that small expenditures and uncontrolled spending habits add up as years pass by. They also know that small savings add up to huge gains the same way. I'm not going to tell you, "Don't smoke, don't drink, don't buy lottery tickets, don't buy Star Bucks, don't buy your daily donut" etc. If an item, hobby or habit brings you genuine joy then you go right ahead and buy it. But remember that the money spent on *that item* is gone—forever—and can't be used for something else.

Monthly charges and premiums add up over time as well. Many of the monthly charges we all pay are necessary evils: Auto insurance, health insurance, homeowners/renters insurance, etc. Increasing your deductable on these policies can reduce your monthly cost by 5%-to-15% or more. Having all of your insurance with one company can result in a multiple policy discount. Reducing your costs means you don't need to earn as much taxable income to pay your bills. Maintain the same income while reducing your costs and you'll have extra money to start a retirement account for yourself. Or you could use that extra money to spend on other worthless items. The choice is yours.

Albert Einstein may not have been a financial genius, but he knew the power of small numbers compounded over time. Let's look at some of these numbers. Numbers show truth. What you do with the numbers is up to you.

Are you a 1-pack a day smoker? 365 packs per year at (conservatively) $6.50 per pack = $2,372.50 annually. Smoke for 5 years and that comes to = $11,862.50 This is providing that cigarettes never go up in price during your smoking career. Had you not smoked and put that same amount into a mutual fund or index fund, at the end of those same 5 years you would be sitting on closer to $13,000 or more. Plus, as a smoker your health insurance premium is more, adding an additional $50 to $100 per month. Stop smoking for one year and your health insurance premium will go down. Then, without ever getting a pay raise, you could be stashing away $2,972.50 per year. Same 5 year period and that equates to $14,862.50 (closer to $16,000 with a conservative 5% rate of return).

Alcohol is another category. Everyone has different drinking habits and the habit evolves or devolves over time. Some people never drank or no longer drink. Most people have no idea of how much they spend/spent on alcohol annually—even social drinkers don't know. In my work in substance abuse I ask that users do an honest accounting of what they spend on booze or drugs. It can be shocking when the real numbers come to light. As I point out to substance users, "You may not drink (or use) every day but you can follow a mathematical equation to figure out what your average daily cost is if you do drink." Let me present this with the aid of some very conservative figures.

You don't drink every day but you do like to go out on weekends. Let's say you spend $50 over the weekend at clubs or bars. (I think most of us can say we've dumped $50 in a bar or have had a bar bill in excess of that while dining out.) 52 X $50 =

$2,600. This equates to an average COST of $7.12 per day. If you also happen to be a smoker then your drinking and smoking "hobby" costs you $13.62 per day to maintain. After 5 years you will have literally burned and pissed through $24,862. If you can afford that and you don't mind spending that kind of money, you go right ahead. But be fully aware that had you put that money into a mutual fund or index fund you would have roughly (and conservatively) $28,000.00 in your account.

My financial situation turned around the very next day after I quit drinking. No, all my bills didn't magically disappear—but I wasn't literally pissing money away anymore and I immediately began paying off my debts. I went from paying off credit card debt, to paying off my car to paying off my home and then to saving and investing money.

Look, I fully support getting pleasure and joy from your money—life is meant to be enjoyed. I don't care if you smoke or drink and I'm not passing along morality here. If your smoking and drinking hobbies bring you joy, who am I to tell you not to do it. My goal is to simply bring mathematical and financial awareness to you. You can still have fun smoking and drinking but a little moderation and conservative usage (which is what I lacked) may help you retain more of your money and build a retirement nest egg.

As a side note here, I must admit that if people didn't drink and smoke as much as they do I wouldn't get those nice juicy dividend checks every 3 months from the beer and tobacco companies that I own stock in. In fact, the more people drink and smoke the more money I make. So I guess I should say, "Please continue smoking and drinking in excess, you're funding my wealthy retirement."

Procrastination can save you money: "You'll never see prices this low again!" Didn't that same car dealer say the same thing last month? This isn't about being patient and waiting for the best price (which isn't a bad idea), this is about waiting and procrastinating to buy something or make a decision to buy something. Had Barry procrastinated a bit before making all of his commitments he wouldn't have ended up as financially strapped. When you procrastinate and DON'T buy something a number of things happen. First, you might eventually discover that you didn't need the item and can survive just fine without it. You didn't impulsively waste money and now you have "unspent" money that you *could* use towards something else. By doing nothing you may have also just saved yourself from committing to 36 monthly payments for something you won't use or really didn't need. You avoided making what eventually may turn out to be a mistake. And who knows, a better or more interesting deal may come along in the meantime. Think how rapidly the price of technology drops once the latest gizmo has been out a few months.

Small expenditures quietly compound and add up. Wealthy people are always looking for ways to trim down their expenses. Not because they're greedy or cheap, it's because wealthy people understand the math behind "Earn more by spending less." Wealthy people value the money they earn and they want to get the most distance and utility out of every penny they spend. Wealthy people know that if they can save $10 on one expense, then that means they have $10 they can apply towards something else, even if that something else is only for fun or enjoyment.

Pay the least amount of taxes allowable by law. Tax evasion is illegal, but proper tax deductions and proper tax planning isn't. Paying the least amount in taxes isn't just smart, it's American! Why pay more than you have to? A lot of people hate the "wealthy" because they supposedly don't pay enough in taxes. According to whom? Wealthy people aren't evil because they look for every tax deduction. Do you want to pay more than your fair share in taxes? Are you evil if you want to pay less in taxes? Seriously, if you earned $1,000,000 in a year would you call the IRS and say, "Um, I think I should pay you more in taxes. Who do I make the check out to and where do I send it?" If you made that kind of money and felt you should pay more then you should donate to needy causes and charitable organizations. (Oooops, that would be a tax deduction. So if you do donate, do it anonymously and don't claim the deduction.)

It is your duty as an American to pay the least amount of taxes allowable by law. This isn't just my opinion, it's the opinion of the U.S. Supreme Court (1976). Tax law is very complicated and there are many "grey" areas. The best thing that regular, hardworking Americans like you and I can do is get tax software and let it walk you through possible deductions. (I use TurboTax.) There are numerous deductions that can help reduce your tax liability. Mortgage interest, property taxes, medical expenses, charitable contributions, work related expenses, child care expenses, tuition loan interest. There are credits and deductions for attending school, for renters and IRA contributions. These are just a few examples.

It's worth the money to buy the latest software and run your own numbers even if you have a service or an accountant prepare your taxes. You should be educated and know what deductions you qualify for. Once you know about certain deductions—and which ones are most beneficial to you—you can do tax planning for next year. You will pay dearly for tax ignorance. It is your duty as an American to pay the least amount of taxes allowable by law. Render unto Caesar what is Caesar's—but not a penny more.

Self-control: Stop yourself once in a while before you buy some random gizmo that looks shiny. Do you really need it? Will it dramatically improve your life? Does it fall into one of your budget categories? Make lists before going to the grocery store, Walmart or wherever you shop. Force yourself to stick to the list on at least one occasion. Put a "smiley face" on the list, place the list on display on the front of your refrigerator and congratulate yourself. Then spend a little time thinking, "Do I really miss, or even remember, what that impulse item was that I didn't buy?

Focused thought: How much do you spend on things? How much money do you need coming in to pay for all these things? Having a budget simplifies these questions. I know exactly how much it costs me to live (comfortably) and I know how much I

99

need to bring in to fulfill my obligations. A budget helps me control impulsive purchases. Without heavy thought I can quickly think, "Is this item part of my budget? If I buy it will I have to sacrifice from a different budget category? Why do I want it? Is it even necessary?" This helps me control making impulsive spending purchases which I'm sure I would regret later.

By establishing a budget, staying on budget and controlling impulsive purchases, I then have money available to do fun, impulsive things—without harming my standard of living or stressing me out. For instance, I like to "impulsively" invite friends out for dinner or I may just pay the entire table's bill at the spur of the moment. I'm not trying to impress or buy friends. If I can afford it, if I'm not using money that should go towards some other obligation and it feels good, I do it. I know that I won't have *that* money to save or invest in the future (and I may have to sacrifice on something else in the future because of my impulsive decision), but I do want to have fun with my money. I want to get the most utility and joy as possible out of it.

Sacrifice: You don't have to live like a martyr, suffering through life eating only figs and fire ants. But you can turn the heat down by a degree or two or turn the A/C up by a degree or two. You can turn the temp down on your water heater by 5 degrees. How big of a sacrifice is it to go with basic cable instead of the full 5-Star package? How big of a sacrifice is it to go with a limited 6 gigabyte data plan instead of the unlimited plan? Is going with a $1000 deductable on your auto insurance instead of $500 or $100 deductable that big of a sacrifice? Can't you sacrifice a little on your car purchase now so you can qualify for (and afford) a 15 year mortgage instead of a 30 year mortgage? Sacrifice mentality will help you think efficiency with your money. Small sacrifices add up to BIG SAVINGS now and over time.

I have been forced to sacrifice during all different periods in my life. I'm sure you have as well. When I couldn't afford steak I had to survive on macaroni and cheese. Now that I can afford steak I still have the *sacrifice mentality*. I don't just grab what looks good,

I look for sales on various cuts of meat and that's what I buy. I don't torture myself but I'm willing to sacrifice a bit in an effort to spend less and then have more money left over for other things.

Look back at Mike and Karen. They might think or feel like they're sacrificing, but they're living and spending to the absolute limits of their income. They aren't building wealth by spending everything they earn. Look back at Jenny and Pete. They earn double what Mike and Karen do, but they're also living at the high limit of what they earn. What if something similar happens to either couple like what happened to Barry? What if one of them loses their job (through no fault of their own), is unable to work or must take a lower paying job? At least Barry had something to fall back on: His IRA and his knowledge and behavior of living with a realistic budget. Barry was and will be in a better position to weather a financial storm than these other two couples.

I'm not trying to instill fear or relay sad stories of doom and gloom. But bad things do happen to good, honest, hardworking people. I would like you to protect your finances, build wealth and build yourself a safety net in the event something inconvenient does happen. Let's hope that nothing financially catastrophic or inconvenient ever does occur in your lifetime. Then you'll really be able to use and enjoy your savings.

Most of what I've talked about here is common sense, but broke people aren't famous for having common sense. You don't need to become a multimillionaire to enjoy your life. A little self-control, focused thought and sacrifice can help YOU make your own life more enjoyable and relaxed. Being broke brings stress upon you. Having a safety net of money, that you don't have to spend simply because it's 'there,' is calming. Self-control, focused thought and sacrifice should be a regular part of your financial and purchasing decisions. Go ahead and have some fun and enjoy your money, but you don't have to buy everything that's in front of you. You don't have to buy everything that's on sale. Reducing what you spend will automatically give you a 'raise' without you having to change careers or put in more hours at your job. Remember that you can earn more by spending less, and that's what genuinely wealthy people do.

Earn more by spending less Worksheet:

Do you think you are always spending more than you should be? If so, on what?_____

As your income increases, do you take on more monthly financial commitments, simply because you have more money?_____

Do you impulsively spend more as your income increases?_____

How and where can you shave 10% off of your monthly expenditures and commitments?_____

What services, features or 'things' can you do without?_____

What will you do to control your spending?_____

Do you regularly check your credit card statements—line by line— to see what you're being charged for?_____

Will you implement a plan to spend less so you can earn more?_____

What will you do with the money you 'save' by spending less?_____

If you do 'stash away' your extra money, where will you put it?_____

Chapter #6

The great delusion.

"Everything will be great when I lose these last 10 pounds."
Really? Why? What changes then?

"**W**on't it be great when... when I get married, get divorced, the kids are grown, I get that new job, I get that new house, I go on vacation, I lose those last 10 pounds, I move to wherever, won't it be great **when I get rich.**" I'm sure you've made a few statements like this, I know I have. Then, when I got there, it wasn't what I thought it would be like or wanted it to be like, and then I found that I wanted something else instead. This is what I call the "Won't it be great when..." delusion.

The feelings we get when we imagine "what it will be like" are often far better than the experience itself. I'm not trying to be a depressing pessimist here, but there is a lot of truth behind this delusion. We imagine things (events, situations, relationships, vacations, jobs, money), will be better than how they actually pan out. However, this is a **good delusion** because it gives us hope and motivates us to make attempts at progress. Quite often when we do reach our goals the experience or final outcome *does* turn out to be just as good, or better than we had imagined. To begin I want to give some examples of the "won't it be great when..." delusion. Don't worry, I'm going to get to all the good, uplifting stuff later in this chapter.

Winning the lottery is a case in point with the, "Won't it be great when..." delusion. Let's say that you dream about winning $1,000,000 in the state lottery, and as luck has it you win! You now have $1,000,000. Will it change your life and be as great as you imagined, or might it be no big deal or actually cause

103

problems? It will all depend on your current financial situation and your own feelings about money. Of course it's wonderful and exciting to win a million dollars, but consider your reference point. If you're already a multi-millionaire, another million would be nice, but not as life changing as if you were poor and won a million dollars.

Let's say you are poor and do win a million dollars. Without doubt your life will change, and in many ways for the better, at first. If you don't plan and figure out how to grow and preserve the money you just won—but just keep on spending it—you won't be a millionaire for very long. Let's say that you do conserve and preserve, but as time passes you become accustom to being a millionaire and you might start demanding more and spending more on luxury items. Even though you haven't earned or worked for your million dollars you might start to feel above those other "poor broke slobs who don't have money." And if you do keep on spending, watching your money dwindle away, you might not feel as good or as excited as you did when you first found out you won or were just dreaming about winning.

I'm not saying that winning a million dollars is bad or that winning the lottery brings the worst out in people. Nor is it that winning or earning a lot of money is a letdown, it's simply a matter that we become accustom to our conditions. As I said in an earlier chapter, "Money changes everything."

Money is a great illustration of the, "Won't it be great when..." delusion. Many people believe that obtaining a lot of money will solve all of their problems. When I hear people make a statement like, "It'll all be great when I'm rich," I come right out and ask: "How much money will make you rich? Tell me the exact amount. By when or by what date? Where will you put it, save it or invest it? Will you spend it? On what? What will you do with what you have left over? How much do you need left over to still be rich? How will you continue bringing in more money to stay rich?" These questions befuddle people because they don't take them into consideration when they make the statement, "Won't it be great when I'm rich." I'm not trying to burst their bubble or deflate their dream, I actually want them to think about these questions so they can help themselves get to where they *think* they want to be.

As a self-proclaimed "Unapologetic Capitalist" I see nothing wrong with earning a good income or winning the lottery and having tons of money. Money absolutely does help improve your standard of living and money is nice to have. But I have also seen some people become extremely rich and NOT become any happier. In fact I have seen some people become more miserable and miserly and some have even gone further into debt as a result of coming into money. Acquiring money has brought on big problems for some people. Don't laugh, it's true. Just watch one of those reality TV shows about lottery winners. (Better yet, instead of watching TV do some research and read articles or studies on lottery winners.) And it's not just lottery winners. Plenty of Rock Stars, Movie Stars and Sports Celebrities have come to ruin due to suddenly having gobs of money. Even Mark Twain went bankrupt because he squandered his money away on get-rich-quick schemes. If you have no plan of what to do with your money once you get it, you'll likely just burn through it and wonder, "Where did it all go?"

As promised, now to some of the uplifting stuff. I'm going to use myself in many examples. I'll tell you about my own behaviors and experiences and I would like you to be able to learn from them. I would like you to think about what you have done in the past, if it was similar and what you'll do in the future to get more utility and higher enjoyment out of your own money and life.

First off, I do dream and I do hold up hope before my mind and think, "Won't it be great when..." If I didn't dream, have hopes and desires then I wouldn't do anything—at least nothing constructive—I would just *react* to whatever happens to me in life.

Let's take this book for instance. I had to *want* to write it, I had to think about it and imagine "Won't it be great when I get another book done? Won't it be great if this book helps people and motivates them to pull themselves out of living broke? Won't it be great if I sell a million copies?" But I didn't imagine this will be the greatest thing I've ever written and that my life will be filled with joy and riches and my life will be complete once I'm done. If I don't earn gobs of money from it I won't view it as a failure, I'll work on something else and I'll keep trying. Even if it does earn me ridiculous amounts of money, I won't stop working and writing. This book is only a part of more things to come.

I don't imagine or expect MORE than I should. I simply want to enjoy the process, enjoy the accomplishment, reflect back on both the process and the accomplishment and then establish a new goal. I'm learning to catch myself before I get too fixated on a destination and then possibly be disappointed once I get there. (I'm using the term "destination" in the larger sense, not just a geographical point.) I have to remind myself to STOP and savor the small accomplishments along the way. I have to STOP and savor the present point which I am at. I try to notice and enjoy the *unfolding* of the event as opposed to expecting the event and its conclusion being the payoff. I don't become delusional simply thinking, "Won't it be great when…" I start *doing* to make the "when" become the experiences of NOW. I can't simply wait around for "when" to happen, I have to make it happen, live it and enjoy the experience of doing it in the NOW.

I have also learned not to demand or expect more from an outcome than is probable or feasible. Quite often I am pleasantly surprised that the outcome **is** great and occasionally it is even **better than** I anticipated. It isn't that I have low expectations— quite the opposite—I have high expectations of myself but I have realistic anticipation of outcomes. By having this type of attitude I'm not disappointed as often because I have a realistic view of outcomes. When I view an undertaking first through the eyes of *feasibility* and then through the eyes of *probability* I find that I experience a higher success rate of accomplishment. Feasibility is asking the question: "Can it happen?" Probability asks the question: "How likely is it that it will happen?"

106

So I use feasibility as part of my "won't it be great when..." thought process. If something is feasible then I believe it's worth attempting and finding out if it will be great or not. I won't know until I try. But I am not so deluded to think that only one single attempt at something will make it happen or that one single event will solve all of my problems and make my life complete. It is the joy of discovery and thinking about what I might experience along the way and then what happens **after** the destination has been reached. So for you, if something is feasible then it might be worth your attempt even if the outcome is not highly probable. Just don't set yourself up for disappointment by expecting too much or expecting a feasible outcome to be a guaranteed outcome.

Once you get "there" (lose the pounds, make the money, buy the house, get married or whatever), that's when other new challenges and changes take place. How will you preserve, maintain and enjoy your new status? How will you keep the weight off? How will you enjoy your new weight? How will you enjoy your new house? How will you enjoy and preserve your wealth?

During the journey is when you work on your plans of what to do once you reach the destination. During the journey is when you practice maintenance and preservation. Planning and practicing can keep you consciously focused and etch your goal deeper into your unconscious mind. You want to be prepared with a practiced plan for when you do reach your goal. Once you hit your goal weight you're not going to start eating like a pig are you? Once you achieve or hit your income or savings goal you aren't going to stop earning and start spending like a drunken sailor are you? If you do eat like a pig and spend out of control you'll just end up back where you were and have to start all over again. Practicing "being there" helps you maintain and preserve what you've gained once you do get there.

Getting through the rough parts of the journey. The journey itself can be a rough road. There can and probably will be plenty of setbacks and disappointments along the way. Most people say, "You just keep at it and it will all work out." That's good advice, but everything doesn't always work out as planned or hoped. I don't know if everything will work out for you as long as you just "keep at it." But I do know this much: **You have ZERO chance of succeeding if you don't try.** I've had my fair share of struggles, I know that it can be very difficult to remember to keep trying and then muster up a forward looking attitude when it appears that everything is going wrong. I am willing to accept a mindset of, "Things don't look good right now but I must keep trying." It's not profound but at least it's true.

Unless something magical or miraculous happens, all destinations require a journey to get there. Some journeys are a struggle and some can be shortened. You can have elective surgery or use pharmaceuticals to obtain weight loss, but you still need to exercise if your desire is to have *genuine* strength and a toned body. You can order a fake diploma online, but you won't have *genuine* knowledge until you study, get hands-on experiences or attend real courses. You can win the lottery or inherit a bunch of money but you will still have to live within financial constraints if you want to maintain *genuine* wealth. You may arrive at your destination rapidly but then the maintenance will become the journey.

Again I return to the truth of mathematics. Your income may be lower than you would like it to be and you may not have many opportunities to advance your income. You may have already cut out every unnecessary expense you can, living on the bare minimums. If you have become buried in debt it may take a lot of sacrifice on your behalf and take a long time for you to dig yourself out of it. Your income may not allow you to live as luxurious a lifestyle as you want to. My dad would always remind me, "You can't live a Champagne lifestyle on a beer budget." None of this may seem fair and balanced. I wish life was fair. A great thinker, speaker and caring man is quoted to have said, "There will always be poor [people]."

I don't believe this man was suggesting that you simply resign yourself to being "poor" and make no effort at improving the living conditions for yourself or your family. I believe his statement was suggesting that you accept reality. The reality is that some people will never put forth any effort to improve their conditions. Some will never conserve or wisely use their limited resource of money. Some will become high income earners yet continue to live broke and in debt. Accept the truth of your own conditions which currently exist, but don't give up. Take it upon yourself to do what you can to make your life better. There will always be poor—but you don't have to be one of them.

Under normal conditions, struggles, sadness and difficulties come and go within a person's life. There are those times, and some of them extended periods of time, where it seems like nothing you do goes right or moves you any closer towards your goals. I have no profound or magic answer for you on this. Sometimes you just have to accept that at this moment, things aren't going your way. Pushing harder and forcing conditions along may be counterproductive during these times. I'm not suggesting you give up or quit, just slow down a bit and allow the journey to unfold. As long as you stay committed to your core productive behaviors you will be keeping yourself in a position to reap the benefits of what you've sown, if or when the tide changes. I offer no guarantee that your tide will change for the better. But the alternative is to just give up and that doesn't seem like a very good option to me, and it shouldn't be to you either.

So with all this in mind, I ask that you never give up on yourself. Please discover your own ways to keep yourself motivated through the rough stretches. Regardless of whether it's weight loss, an education or building wealth—it's all a journey. Be an active participant and director of your journey. What has helped me enjoy life's journeys more is that I don't expect too much from a final destination and I don't view missing a final destination (or goal) as failure. Failure isn't defined by not achieving an outcome that you desired, failure is not even trying.

Investment or purchase? I feel that this topic is relevant to the discussion of delusions. There is a distinct difference between an investment and a purchase. Again you say, "Duh, I know this Mark." But many people confuse the two or use mental accounting deception to justify a purchase as being an investment. I'm not saying that you shouldn't buy fun things or ever make frivolous purchases, but being honest about which is which may help you make wiser purchases or fewer purchases cloaked as investments.

For instance, let's consider what's really going on when you buy a house. While one may call it an investment it is actually a purchase, unless you bought the property with the intent of renting it out (or renting out part of it in the case of a duplex or townhouse), or that you fully intend on selling it at a certain price by a certain date. You might think that your personal residence is an investment, but it's really a purchase.

With your primary home you can count on maintenance costs and various improvement costs. Improvement and remodeling costs will be considerably different between an investment property and your personal residence. You may undertake remodeling and upgrades in your home because of your own personal desires and tastes. You can tell yourself that certain improvements are an investment towards increasing the selling price (like Jenny & Pete's hot tub). But many improvements and upgrade costs will not be recouped in the sale of your private residence. No real estate is guaranteed to increase in value. Market conditions or changing neighborhood conditions are out of your direct control. Your personal residence may be worth the same amount or less than you paid for it when you sell it.

However, even if you do sell your primary home for the same price or less than you paid for it you have likely still gained. You have to pay to live somewhere, so in essence you have been paying rent to yourself. This may sound like a mental accounting trick but it is a mathematical truth. If you pay $800 per month to live in an apartment you have amassed nothing at the end of your stay. If you pay the same amount towards a mortgage (principal and interest), you are reducing the amount you owe and building your equity. If you sell your home for the same amount that you paid, you will receive your down payment money back along with any equity you have built through reducing your mortgage balance. Even if you sell your home for less than what you paid, you should end up with some money back in your pocket. This is NOT always the case. People have had to sell their home for MUCH less than they paid or have been foreclosed on because they couldn't make the payments. That's when a home is clearly a money losing purchase and NOT an investment. But even if you do take a loss on the sale of your property you would have been able to take advantage of positive tax deductions (interest and property taxes) while you were living there. So—in my opinion—your personal residence is a *wise purchase* as opposed to a clear-cut investment.

An investment means that you will pay a certain amount for something today and you intend to sell it in the future (on or by a determined date for a higher price), or at any moment for a higher price than you paid for it. But an investment is not realized until a transaction takes place (you sell it). The only time you profit on an investment is when you sell it for more than you paid. Even if your investment is gaining in value it is only a *holding* until a sales transaction takes place. You can borrow (margin or leverage) against your holdings, but an actual gain or loss does not exist (become realized) until a sales transaction has taken place.

A purchase means that you will either consume the product you have bought or you *may* sell it at some future point, knowing that you will likely receive less than what you paid or have totally spent on it. A car, boat or RV would be examples of this. You are purchasing utility, not making an investment. You don't get your money back for all the gas you bought while using it. A truck which is specifically used for work can technically be considered an investment. A bulldozer or other work machines are investments. It's easy to determine if something is an investment— if it qualifies as a tax expense or can be depreciated, it's an investment. You **can't** expense or depreciate your personal car on

111

your taxes, but you may be able to claim a mileage deduction on your taxes if you use your car to perform your job.

I have purchased plenty of "Big Boy" toys and ended up selling them for far less than I paid or had hoped to sell them for. When I was younger I would delude myself into thinking that the 'toy' I was buying was an investment. I overspent and bought a lot of toys that I didn't need or I got very little use (utility) out of. But I've learned. I no longer confuse 'purchase' with 'investment'. I know that if I'm buying a toy today I may sell it someday in the future at a lower price. This helps me make what I believe to be wiser decisions with my toy purchases. I ask myself, "How much fun and enjoyment will I get now and in the foreseeable future? Will the fun and enjoyment be worth the price I must pay now? Am I willing to sell my toy for far less than I am paying now? Can I afford to take that kind of financial loss?" If the answer is "yes," I then move closer towards making the purchase or I begin my negotiation process.

Be very mindful of the difference between a purchase and an investment. Don't talk yourself into thinking one is the other. Salespeople will do that for you. If you plan on reselling something at a profit by a certain date, at a specific price, or when you get the right offer, then it is an investment. You can be emotionally tied to your purchases but you must be emotionless towards your investments. If you're emotionally tied to an investment you will likely demand or want more for it than the market is willing to pay and then you may end up losing money on an investment.

For example if you bought a home for investment purposes and ended up doing a lot more work on it than you thought you would have to, you'll want more money for it when you sell it. If you did a lot of the repairs and upgrades yourself, you feel emotionally tied to it and your labor and sweat equity are worth asking more. "I did all this work myself, I left a lot of my skin and blood on this property. It's worth every penny I'm asking for it." It doesn't matter to the buyer who did the work (providing that it was done correctly). As a buyer, I don't care what this property means to you

112

or how much you spent on repairs and upgrades or how much you feel your work is worth. All I care about is the market value and what it's worth to me right now.

"But I put in all new plumbing and had to replace all the drywall." Well, that's your problem. Why did you buy a house that needed new plumbing and drywall? I want to buy a house that's ready for occupancy. Thanks for doing all that work, but no matter what it cost YOU, all we have here is a house that's up to livable standards, and all I'm willing to pay for it is market value.

Every investment doesn't make you money and every purchase doesn't bring you as much joy as you thought it would. Every investment, even if it does make you money, doesn't always bring you happiness.

"Do you know what I'm worth?" is another delusion. Let's say you bought 1,000 shares of Apple stock years ago for $85 each ($85,000). After accounting for dividend reinvestment and splits you have 9,118 shares and now Apple stock is trading at $115 a share. Your "worth" is huge ($1,048,570). You have a 1,172% return on your original investment of $85,000 but your actual spendable money on hand has not increased. You can't buy food, pay the utilities or make a car payment with your worth, you need real money for that. But many people tend to be fooled and begin spending up to their "worth" by purchasing things with loans and taking on debt.

People can be deluded by their worth, but worth isn't readily spendable money—only money is money. "What I'm worth" is your safety nest egg—it's what you plan on living off of in your retirement or have in case of emergency. That's what gives you the feeling of security. You can always sell off some of your worth to get money to go buy something, or in an emergency you can sell some of that Apple stock to get your hands on cash. But your "worth" will then be reduced by the amount you took out. Technically you can spend your worth or reinvest it, but that's only if you margin and leverage against your value. We'll discuss how and why some people do this in chapter #11.

People also get upset, if not downright ill when they see their portfolio or worth lose value. Let's go with the Apple stock as an example. You have 9,118 shares and Apple stock is trading at $115, giving you a worth of $1,048,570. If Apple stock goes down and it's now trading at $86 per share, your worth has dropped by $264,422. That's not pretty to look at, but you haven't lost any real money. You won't get a bill from your broker asking for $264,422. You're total worth is just lower (now you're only worth $784,148). Even if you panic and sell it all, you wouldn't have lost money, you would still have a giant profit, you simply made less.

Losses are emotionally more disproportionate than gains. Leaving money on the table, getting less than you thought you would or taking a real loss brings higher anxiety than the actual dollar amount is worth. Gaining $10 feels great, but losing $1 feels worse and more intense than the joy of gaining $10. Many behavioral and psychological studies have been done on this strange disproportionate loss emotion. This loss emotion is illogical but it's true.

Let me give you an example. Let's say I'm planning to buy 1,000 shares of Fart-Co at $12 apiece. The shares tick down to $11.80 and I buy the stock and the stock goes back up to $12 after I bought it. Wow what a lucky break for me to get in at a lower price than I was willing to pay and I'm already up $200 (in value only). Then the stock continues to go up the next day and I sell my shares for $13 apiece. I made $1,180.10 in **real money**! (I had an expense of $19.90 in & out commission.) The stock keeps going up to $13.38 after I sold it and I grumble that, "I missed out on $380" but I remind myself that I did make almost $1,200. But what makes me feel even better is that by the end of the day Fart-Co stock has dropped back to $12.50 a share—.50 cents less than what I sold it for. Boy do I feel smart and happy—I feel like a stock market genius. Until the next day when I happen to see in the business news that Fart-Co is being bought out by Bean Brothers

Corporation for $15 a share. Now I'm pissed. I'm all upset because I *could have* made another $2,000 if I had just waited. (But I had no knowledge of this buyout by Bean Brothers, no one did.) I forget how happy I was after I made $1,200 and all I can think about is how much I missed out on. In fact, I *feel* like I lost money, even though I made money.

We have a multitude of issues here. First off, I was apparently too emotionally tied to the investment (stock) or I wouldn't have been watching for news on the company after I had sold it. That's like looking at pictures of old lovers and pining over them. They're gone so you need to get over it and move on. But on the other hand, if I can stay emotionally detached from the investment (stock in this case), I can keep watching it to see if there's another opportunity to buy and sell it again. We can have an ongoing relationship, kind of like "Friends with *financial* benefits." The biggest error I am guilty of is feeling angry and upset (at who knows what) because I missed out on making more. That feeling of anger clouds the important fact that I had made **real money** off the trade and this irrational "I missed out" emotion takes the joy out of the profiting emotion.

How is this relevant? The "If only I would have…" delusion is the same confusing mental trickery as the "Won't it be great when…" delusion. Neither statement takes facts or reality into account. When we look back at "If only I would have…" saved more, waited longer, planned better, invested more, not gotten married, got married, not gotten divorced, got divorced, took that other job, whatever, all we are doing is torturing ourselves and living in a delusion. How do we know how the, "If only I would have…" situation might have turned out? It could have turned out worse than where we *think* we are now.

All we have to go on are the facts and conditions that exist NOW. You can and should learn from past mistakes, but who's to say they were even mistakes? Maybe they were just unlucky events that occurred at inopportune times? You made decisions at the time which you thought were the right decisions to make, even if it was marrying the wrong person, wasting money on dumb stuff or living *beyond* your income and without a budget. You did it because you wanted to and because you thought it was right—at the time.

Actual money is measured in mathematical truth, but a big part of enjoying money, and even becoming wealthy, is psychological. What's important is that you try to see your own mental flaws and errors, then try to correct them and try not to exhibit the same behavior again. You only rob yourself when you stop trying. Do what you can to ground yourself in reality instead of overly emotional or delusional thinking. The point here isn't to get you to become a cold, critical financial thinker. The point is to help you be calmer and not let emotions cloud your financial decisions. I would like you to be better at setting and achieving goals—to persevere on your path even when the path gets rough. I also hope that you will be a bit wiser knowing the difference between investments and purchases. This will help you enjoy your purchases more and help you enjoy any of the gains you may get from an investment.

Financial delusions Worksheet

Of all the delusions mentioned here, do you feel you fall prey to any of them? Which ones?_____

How do you think you can better handle these delusions?_____

Have you ever made a *purchase* while telling yourself it was an *investment*?_____

Do you think you will know the difference between a purchase and an investment in the future?_____

Do you think that knowing the difference between a purchase and an investment will change your buying habits?_____

Do you get more upset over a $1 loss than the joy you feel from a $10 gain? If so, why?_____

Do you emotionally misinterpret a missed opportunity or money left on the table as a loss?_____

Do you ruminate over "if only I would have..."?_____

What will you do to control these emotions and try to be more grateful and calmer in the future?_____

Chapter #7

Does saving money make you happy?

"Someday I'll save for the future…" Sorry, but the future is right now!

There are two distinct definitions to the term, "saving money." One of the definitions refers to a savings in cost. We *save money* off of the purchase price of an item. When a $10 item is reduced to $5 we *save money* on the purchase. By spending less than we thought we would have to pay for an item or service—less than what we felt was either a fair market price or its original marked "anchor" price—we are *saving money*. Using coupons and rebates is an example of this. Buying pre-owned, demos, floor models or shopping at resale shops are other examples. But this type of *saving money* still requires **spending** money.

We also *save money* by **not buying** something, by **not spending** any money. This is when you avoid making a purchase, either by choice or because you didn't need to. "I was going to buy a new HDTV because they were on sale, but I just bought this one 2 years ago and it looks fine. So I saved the money instead." Or "I thought I would need to get the air conditioner repaired on my car but I checked the fuses and all it needed was a new fuse. I saved a ton of money."

Another way of *saving money* is by **not spending** through consciously conserving resources—by using less of a resource that you have to pay for—electricity, gasoline or any other consumable that through your own effort you use less of. For instance, driving less, carpooling or better planning to combine driving errands are examples for using less gas. Turning the A/C up or the heat down a couple of degrees is using less of a resource that you will have to pay for. Repurposing something is another example of *saving money*. "I used the lumber from that shed I tore down to do the deck repairs. It looks great and I didn't have to buy any new wood. I saved myself about 50 bucks."

Doing your own repairs and employing your own labor can fall into this *saving money* category. Washing your own clothes, cleaning your own house/apartment, mowing your own lawn, doing your own oil changes or home maintenance are examples. You're still spending some money, but you're using the resource of yourself, hence **not paying** someone else to do these services for you. But if you don't have the skills, doing something yourself can end up costing you more in the long run. We'll dissect this in chapter 8.

I'm a big fan of all these strategies for *saving money*. Using coupons is fun, providing it's a coupon for something I normally buy or consume. Conserving resources is just plain smart. Why spend more for anything than you have to? But my personal favorite is **repurposing**. I get so much joy out reusing lumber, hardware, extra parts, whatever. This feels good on multiple levels. I haven't wasted a resource by throwing it away. I'm reducing garbage and when I find an item that I've inventoried that I can repurpose, that means I don't have to spend more money, or my time, going to buy more stuff that I don't need. And by staying out of stores I'm not going to fall prey to impulse purchases either. "I came here to buy a 2x4 but look, they have those cool shiny things on sale so I better get one."

All of these *money saving* strategies can bring short-term feelings of happiness. However, saving money may also bring long-term feelings of happiness if a strategy was used towards a major purchase such as a home, car, boat or something that you'll enjoy over an extended period of time. Buying demos, floor models, closeouts, preowned and distressed real-estate are examples. Private purchases don't come with warrantees, but most retailers offer the same guarantee and warranty on demos or previously opened items. Always ask if a demo is available for purchase and if it it's covered by the same guarantee and warranty.

Saving money on purchases can become a way of life for some people and this can bring steady happiness to them. Using coupons, buying only what's "on sale," looking for bargains and finding what they feel is the best deal brings people happiness and feelings of self-worth. Like most things in life there is a learning curve. But once you've learned the process and built it into your way of life it becomes easy and less time consuming.

I want to tell you about my friend Lisa, she is truly amazing at saving money through using coupons, discounts and all sorts of creative points programs. Lisa actually **makes money by shopping**. I learned a lot of strategies from her that I now use.

First off, Lisa and her husband Bob live a very comfortable life. They are medium level income earners, but they live so well because of Lisa's money saving practices. Lisa spends a couple hours of her time every week browsing newspapers and flyers for traditional paper coupons. She is specifically looking for coupons that are good towards products and product types that she normally buys. She has also discovered free websites that simplify finding coupons and bargains. These websites provide links for printable coupons so she doesn't have to go searching for them. (There are too many sites to list here and some sites are regional. Just do a google search for "coupons" and you'll find plenty.)

Lisa also uses multiple coupons towards a single item. She will use a manufacturer's coupon along with a store coupon towards a box of cereal for example. If it's an in-store "Buy one get one free" offer, she will check one of her favorite coupon websites to see if there's a manufacturer coupon. If there is a manufacturer's coupon she will print up 2 coupons—one for each item in the "buy one get one free" offer—making the final price for both items even lower. Yes, you can use a coupon for each item in a 2-for-1 purchase.

Lisa has been introduced to many new products and new manufacturers through her use of coupons. Some of these new products and companies have replaced her old favorites. She has found that new companies, along with well-established companies, will offer coupons with dramatic discounts on their newest products to get consumers to try them.

Lisa has also found a bunch of "Apps" that she uses to build credit points for buying products. None of these Apps cost anything. Many of the Apps are with major retailers where she normally shops. (CVS, Walgreen's, Walmart, Target, to mention a few). When she buys a "qualified" item she scans the barcode and her receipt, and then she receives "points." Most of the store Apps then offer in-store credits. She uses those credits towards future "qualified" items and just keeps rebuilding her points. She has also found other Apps that require the same steps (scan the barcode and receipt), but those points can be redeemed for **cash**. She currently had $43 waiting on one App and $26 waiting on another. Once she surpasses $50 she has the money dropped into her checking account. Again, these are all products or product types that she would normally buy. She has enough self-control to not buy items she doesn't need or wouldn't use.

What about security? "I'm diligent about watching my accounts. It only takes a few seconds to check and see if any weird transactions have taken place. I've never been hacked. I'm sure some company is collecting data on my shopping habits, but so what? You're being tracked virtually anywhere you browse on the internet." What about spam or junk email? "I think it's safe to say that everybody gets spam and junk email. I know who credible sources of email are. I don't open unfamiliar emails and I simply delete the rest. Oh sure I get plenty of unsolicited discounts and coupons, but most of them are for products I've bought before or from manufacturers I trust. Their systems are really smart. They know what I like and what I normally buy. They're actually saving me time by sending me the coupons, I don't have to go look for them. And that's how I end up getting to use multiple coupons on a single item."

I'm sure you're curious, just as I was, to ask, "Exactly how much do you save off purchases? Exactly how much do you earn from all of these points programs and in-store credits?" Let's go with the cash back Apps first. Lisa can see her current total for the year and her entire history total. If she collects more than $600 cash back in a year from an individual site she will receive a 1099 and that amount will need to be reported as income on her taxes. She's vigilant to stay just under $600 on each of the cash back sites she uses. Lisa uses 2 Apps and the same purchase is often "qualified" for each App. Even if all she earns in cash back is $500 per year from each App site that's $1,000 for the year. The same $600 threshold applies to in-store credits. As long as she stays below $600 she doesn't receive a 1099. So even if she shops at only one grocery store, one drug store and two general merchandise stores, she can earn another $2,000 per year just for buying what she would normally buy. She typically **earns** well over $3,000 a year just for using coupons, participating in programs and being a smart shopper.

How much money does she *save* annually on food, clothing, bath, health products, home goods and other essential purchases? She doesn't have an exact figure for that. She *could* give us that figure if she wanted to input every single purchase, discount, coupon, rebate and point reward into a spreadsheet software program. (A lot of stores already do this for you, showing right on the receipt what your savings were for today's purchases, year to date and total since joining or signing up for their discount card.) What's more important than knowing the exact amount she has *saved* is what she does with the pennies that she **has not spent**. Like me, she has a budget and anything left over (not spent) in a budget category gets transferred to her Money Market account at her brokerage.

But just for the sake of example, it's not out of the realm of probability to say that Lisa saves more than $50 each time she goes grocery shopping, which is once a week. She easily fills her cart with $100 worth of food and personal products. But after coupons, discounts, 2-for-1, etc., she hands the cashier $30 to $40 (or less) for everything. We can conservatively say that she *saves* over $2,600 per year off the price of products she needs to survive and would normally be buying anyway. This brings her total annual savings/earnings to $6,000 (or more). And that savings/earnings is then placed into her Money Market account. Make this a regular routine and you can see how after a few years of doing this you can amass a lot of money. That's how normal, working-class people become wealthy!

A few chapters back I spouted off on how it's your duty as an American to pay the least amount of taxes allowable by law. The beautiful benefit of using coupons and getting discounts is that you don't pay income taxes on money you saved off of a purchase. You don't pay income taxes on rebates, cash back and in-store credits, providing that they are under a specific dollar amount for the year. (The recognized amount is $600 but check the "terms" on the sites and services you use, they may send you a 1099 regardless of the amount.) And if you ever do receive a 1099 you MUST report it as income no matter how small the amount.

At the close of my interview Lisa told me, "Most people don't want to spend the time to do research or to learn. But once you've learned and make something part of your regular routine it becomes easier and requires less time. I have so much fun looking for bargains and saving money."

Lisa's right. I hear people say, "I don't have time for all that. My time is more valuable than to spend it hunting for coupons to save a nickel on a box of rice." But Lisa doesn't spend her life searching for nickel coupons. She had to go through a learning curve, but now she has her process fine-tuned and it doesn't take up all that much of her time. She still goes out to see movies and enjoys dinners at restaurants with her husband Bob. (Using Groupon.com and LivingSocial.com discounts they've discovered new theatres and restaurants they never would have tried.) Lisa has a fulltime job and still enjoys her evenings relaxing and weekends playing in her garden or lounging around their pool. They certainly don't live like paupers. Their life is about getting the most mileage out of every penny they spend.

You may not want to spend the time to find coupons and learn how to save. But remember the math: 20 nickels becomes a dollar. And by accumulating one million individual dollars—one at a time—you become a millionaire. If you say, "I don't have time for all that." All I can say is, "Then I guess you don't want to save money and become a millionaire that badly do you?"

Returns and refunds are another big money saving strategy. If you're not satisfied with a product, if it broke or you discover that you have no need for it, why not return it? You might think, "Of course I return things that break," but you would be surprised at how many people don't. Or people don't request a credit when something they recently purchased is suddenly on sale, or ask for a credit when something you recently purchased is suddenly on sale. Many of you probably do this but a majority of people don't.

There are plenty of reasons people don't follow through on returns and sales price refunds. Usually it's time. "I don't want to stand around waiting in line for a $2 credit (or return a $10 item). My time is worth more than that." I agree that your time is valuable and worth money, but that's what we're talking about here—YOUR money. So what if you have to stand in line and putz around for 10 minutes to get a $19 refund or a $5 credit, isn't YOUR money and time worth that much?

Another reason is that people feel foolish or intimidated when making returns. People don't like confrontation so they avoid returning items. But it doesn't have to be confrontational and it probably won't be. The *thought* that it will be a confrontation is enough to stop a lot of people from making a return. If the store has a "Satisfaction Guaranteed" return policy then all you have to say is, "I wasn't satisfied." Or just say, "It turns out I can't use it."

You don't have to go into long, detailed explanations or argue with the returns clerk.

Another reason for not returning something is that people don't save their receipt or packaging materials. You don't have to be a hoarder, but open the package neatly and make sure it works as advertised or that it at least suites your needs or standards. If the product works and you're pleased with it, then recycle the packaging. Most stores will accept a return even if it's not in the original package. Decide how you want to organize your receipts. You can organize them by store or by month. The simplest is to have 12 folders, one for each month. When you buy a product just toss the receipt into the current month's folder. As you start a new month you'll come across last year's receipts. Throw them out if you no longer need them. This isn't as time consuming as you think and it doesn't have to be a fancy filing system but it will help you when you might need to return something. If you don't feel like doing this then don't, but this is YOUR money we're talking about here.

Don't hesitate to return items that you're not satisfied with or that you won't use. Stores expect a certain number of returns—that's why they have a "Returns Counter." Don't give stores any more of your money than you need to. Why should they earn a profit on something you don't like or won't use? You spend plenty of money and you are a valuable customer. When you have a hassle-free return you're likely to shop at that store again in the future.

Sale price credits. Most stores have a policy of crediting you back the sales price difference if you bought the item within the past 10 days. However, if you've had it longer than 10 days you can be smart enough to work around this. Most stores have a 90 day return policy. I have no problem asking for a credit if I see the same item on sale within 90 days of me buying it. You can just pleasantly ask, "I know I'm past the 10 day limit, but can you at least give me an in-store credit on the difference?" The clerk often will. If they hesitate or say, "I'm sorry, our policy is 10 days on sale price credits," I come right out and ask nicely, "What would YOU do if it were YOUR money?" A lot of times this gets them thinking and they oblige my request for an in-store credit. If you get no cooperation then look at the return policy. If it's a 90 day return policy, then return the item you purchased for a full refund and go buy a new one at the sale price. Or, buy a new one that's on sale, go out to your car, grab the receipt from the original purchase and return the one you just bought using the higher priced receipt. (I call this a "Receipt Swap.") Is this a pain and a hassle? A little, but we're talking about YOUR money here.

If you don't want to go through the "buy and return" process then ask for the manager and directly tell them what you intend to do—that you will return your original item or do a receipt swap. The manager doesn't want open boxes or returned items so they will often "override" the system and offer you an in-store credit. At least a smart store manager will do this.

I received over $200 credit back to my account during a 90 day period as I watched the price of an HDTV I had recently purchased keep dropping. I asked for a credit twice during this period. Each time I had to speak with the manager and each time I said, "I don't care if I have to go home and get the TV and return it. $100 is a lot of money to me. And I'm sure you don't want to try and sell a used TV."

I made the same credit request for a snow thrower I had purchased from a national hardware store. I had purchased the snow thrower less than a month prior (29 days) when I saw that they had marked the same snow thrower down by an additional $150 for the end of the season. I asked for a credit back to my account. The returns clerk didn't know what to do because I had purchased a floor model. The manager wasn't cooperative at all. The manager told me, "You bought a floor model. Our sale credit policy is within 10 days of purchase and you've had it for more than 10 days." I pointed out that their return policy for power equipment (even on floor models) was 90 days and I could return it for a full refund. Then he got a bit snotty with me, "What, you're going to go all the way back to your house, load it into a truck and bring back a used snow thrower?" I walked away from the counter and that's exactly what I did. After the return was done I asked for the same manager. I told him, "Congratulations. You now have a used snow thrower that you can try to sell—next winter." I believe I heard him making an appeal to me as I walked away but it was too late. Do you think I will ever shop at that hardware chain again? No.

Stash it away!

Saving money on purchases reduces your outflow of cash. Avoiding purchases, not spending money, repurposing and employing your own labor also reduces your outflow of cash. Asking for sales credits and returning items you don't like or don't use reduces your outflow of cash. These are all part of the process of earning more by spending less. But when you have spent less or avoided spending, what do you do with those saved pennies? This takes us to the next definition of saving money.

This definition of "saving money" is the act of stashing it away. How or where you stash it away is up to you. Some like to stash cash, some like acquiring stocks, bonds or put it into a savings account. A bank savings account is the most common reference for "saving money." Having a savings account helps you feel calmer to face the unknown. It also gives you a feeling of pride, independence and for some, feelings of self-worth.

Quite a few interviews and studies have been done on the subject of having a *savings account* and that having one brings people happiness. It's questionable whether stashing money away in a savings account brings someone *genuine happiness* or not, but these studies purport that having a savings account does bring happiness to people. In these particular studies and interviews people use the word "happiness," but I believe that maybe the word they really should be using is "security." When you feel secure you are calmer and when you're calm you're generally happier. If you're curious you can check the archives of any business newspaper or financial magazine for articles on this subject.

However, both spending less and stashing money away can become an obsession. The obsession can turn from happiness into frustration, compulsion or unhealthy behaviors. Some people end up starving themselves and their family (figuratively and literally). Some people become so obsessed with spending less money that they will forgo products and services which would make theirs and their family's life much more pleasant or healthier. They could easily afford some comforts without affecting their financial security, but they're too obsessed with amassing money to spend any of it. "If I spend less money I can stash more money away."

I'm certainly not implying that saving on purchases or stashing money away is unhealthy or will lead to an obsession. A fun and comfortable balance needs to be found. As I said in the beginning of this book, what's the point of scrimping, saving and denying yourself your favorite Starbucks just to finally crack open the vault and have Starbucks in the waning years of your life.

What is that balance? There is no "fixed" amount that you must save. Financial gurus spout out all kinds of figures. "You need to have 1.2 million to retire. You need to have 6 months of wages saved for an emergency." Well what if you don't need 1.2 million to retire on? What if you have plans for a simple life in retirement? Or what if you currently spend more than you earn? Then saving 6 months wages won't be enough. What if you spend less than you earn? Then 6 months wages is more than sufficient and may be overkill. Let's look at both of these, saving for retirement and saving for an emergency. We'll go over emergency savings first.

Emergency Savings: Rule-of-thumb is that you should have 6 months wages saved up—in a readily accessible savings account— for in the event that you get laid off, injured or are unable to work for whatever reason. But what if you're a high-earner and a big spender? Your monthly obligations and expenses may be higher than your wages. Then that 6 month wage equation doesn't work and after a couple of months of unemployment you'll be strapped for cash or start defaulting on bills. Instead, you may want to **save an amount equal to 6 months of your expenses**. "Well I don't know what my expenses are or what they might be." If you were following a budget you would know that precise amount.

This same 6 months of expenses applies towards someone who spends below their income. In this situation if you saved 6 months of wages in a bank savings account, but your expenses were lower, you would have more money than necessary sitting in a bank savings account underperforming. That excess money could be earning a higher interest or getting you a higher return in some other financial instrument (U.S. Savings Bonds, Money Market or equities).

There are a few more things to consider. Where do you want your "Emergency Account" held? If it's in an IRA or your 401(K) and you need to access it, it will cost you a lot and not just in money. At the very least you will pay .30 cents for every $1 you need. This is because that money was pre-tax. So you will have to pay a 10% early withdrawal penalty and then pay taxes on the money. Additionally this can be a real accounting nightmare because the taxes aren't automatically deducted when you redeem from an IRA or 401(K). You'll have to hang on to some money to pay the tax on it at the end of the tax year.

It's unrealistic to access money from these type of accounts every 2 weeks or every month to pay off bills. You'll need to plan ahead and figure out how long you expect to be out of work and how much you'll need, then take a large withdrawal. Then if you are lucky enough to land a job in the next few weeks, and you don't need the rest of the money you've withdrawn, what do you do with it? It would be foolish to put it back into your IRA (you've already paid a penalty and taxes).

So for example, if you figure that you'll need $5,000 to pay your bills you will have to request a withdrawal of $7,000+. Here's how the math works:

$7,000 IRA Withdrawal
-$700 Early withdrawal penalty
-$1,400 Taxes to be paid (estimate)
$4,900 is what you're left with

I suggest that the best place to "hold" emergency money is in a bank savings account, Money Market account or in an index fund through a brokerage. You can access the money easily and in smaller increments as needed. There will be no early withdrawal penalties and the tax implications will be small, if any at all. A savings account offers the lowest interest return, but the money is always there and it won't lose any value. A Money Market fund offers a slightly higher interest return, it won't lose any value but there may be certain limitations (3-day hold on funds, $2,500 minimum balance requirement or it's only accessible during regular banking hours). An index fund can lose value and it might be worth less per share when you happen to need the money in an emergency. But if you can handle a bit of risk then put your "Emergency money" into index funds.

We can't decide when accidents, emergencies and inconveniences happen—they **always** happen at the worst time. That's why it's comforting to have 6 months' worth of expenses stashed away. My friend Jennifer was on a cross-country road trip when she had car trouble and needed over $800 in repairs. She paid for the repairs with her credit card and when she returned home withdrew the money from her emergency fund to pay off the card balance. While the road trouble was an inconvenience, the payment of the repairs wasn't financially painful and it didn't throw a wrench into her standard of living. She had to admit, "I'm so glad I had that emergency fund sitting there. I was able to continue with my travel plans and enjoy the rest of my trip without worrying about how I was going to pay for all this. Now I just have to slowly rebuild my emergency balance." This is coming from someone who had always lived a paycheck-to-paycheck lifestyle, didn't think about savings and never had an emergency fund before she was 40. It's never too late to start your own emergency fund.

Emergency and unexpected expenses may not happen in your life or they may be infrequent. But then again, you may have more than your fair share of bad luck and unexpected emergencies. There is no "fair share"; I'm using it as a figure of speech. But what if you do happen to end up unemployed, sick or injured for 8 months or more? After you've drained your emergency fund (if you have one), you might be tempted to withdraw out of your 401(K) or IRA (if you have either of those). DON'T! Act like they don't exist. You may have to make some unpleasant adjustments to your lifestyle, sell off some of your belongings or accept a low paying or part-time job. But if you're creative and tenacious you will rebuild your life, dealing with and working around these new limitations which exist.

Let me repeat that under NO CIRCUMSTANCES should you ever dip into your IRA or 401(K). Some people will disagree with me and I admit that there may be certain situations where you must draw out of them (costly medical emergencies, terminal health). But barring these types of situations, if you do dip into either one of them, you'll be calling me in 18 months whining about how much tax you owe, that you don't have the money to pay your taxes and now your retirement account is depleted. Don't get mad when I say, "I told you so." Your IRA and 401(K) are like Super Models—the figures are fun and pleasing to look at but you aren't allowed to touch them—not until you've both aged and matured, then you can play with them all you want.

Now that you're at least thinking about an "Emergency Account" I would like YOU to decide how much you need saved to feel safe. This will get you involved in your own financial future and make this a very personal process. You may not feel the need to have very much saved for an emergency ($500) or you may feel that you need a specific dollar amount saved ($5,000). Only YOU know what amount will put your mind at ease. The amount you need saved will likely change during the course of your life and I can literally guarantee that at some point in your life you'll be glad you have that account. Life doesn't ask you what you want or hold off with problems until it's a convenient time for you.

Across all of these studies and interviews, everyone who had some type of savings account said that they were happier than when they didn't have any savings. It's hard to say if they are *genuinely happy*, but they are likely calmer and have fewer financial anxieties. Having your own "emergency account" will help you feel this same type of calmness. And this takes us to our next topic.

How much do I need to save to retire wealthy?

This actually sparks more questions than answers. How much you'll need for retirement depends on your current age and at what age you want to retire. Will you be continuously employed between now and retirement? Will you continue earning the same amount? Will you be able to satisfy all of your debts before retirement? You may be forced into retirement sooner than you plan and still owe on a mortgage or some other loan. You may want to work part-time in retirement but your health or mobility may not allow for it. If you're married does your spouse work or have an income? Will he/she retire at the same time? It also depends on what you hope to do in retirement, whether you want to travel, how and where you might want to travel (in your own car, an RV or by plane?). You may want or need to downsize your home and move into a retirement community or condo. No one can guess how many years you'll live after retirement. I don't mean to sound morbid but these are truths. There are so many variables and uncertainties that it's difficult to answer exactly how much you will need. But that doesn't mean you shouldn't plan for it.

We all have different desires for our retirement and we all have different opinions of how much is enough because **we all have**

different values for money and wealth. So how much money do you need to save so you can retire happily? I don't know and neither do you. This may not be the answer you were expecting. You might have been hoping that I was going to tell you an exact dollar amount. I will however make some suggestions, after I ask a few more questions.

What type of retirement life do you dream of? Is it a realistic dream considering your current interests, health, physical abilities and earning power? No matter how much money you save up it's unrealistic to think that you can retire and go ski the mountain ranges of the world if you're overweight and physically inactive. Or regardless of how physically fit you are it's unrealistic to think you can retire to a beach-front home in Hawaii and surf every day if you don't even have enough money saved to buy a plane ticket to get there. Your dream retirement may be to hang out at your lake cabin and go fishing with your grandchildren. That style of retirement won't be as expensive as traveling the world. Once you have an idea of what kind of life you want to lead and what you want to do, then you'll have a better idea of how much you'll need to save up.

But if you really insist that I give you a dollar figure I'll suggest one. Shoot for **one million dollars** in combined assets and savings. That might sound like an astronomical figure to you but at least you'll have a goal. Even if you only get half way there, $500,000 can make for a darn comfortable retirement. Is that amount impossible? Not really. Most of us will earn—over our lifetime— around one million dollars. Most of us will work for at least 40 years or more (age 25 thru 65). If you buy a home, pay off the mortgage before retirement, save and invest 10% to 15% of your earnings during your working years (more if you don't buy a home), **you can** amass around $500,000 in combined assets and savings. Instead of calling it Retirement Savings or Retirement Fund, why not rename it your "Living Fund." Just a thought. So set your retirement goal for combined assets and savings at $1,000,000. If you only get half way there, that'll be pretty good.

To make this all possible, you have to spend less than you bring in. Use the *money savings* strategies we discussed in the beginning of this chapter. Look for bargains, use coupons and discounts. Don't hesitate to return things you don't use and be willing to ask for credits back. Don't give stores and businesses any more of your money than you have to. Live pleasantly but frugally. As long as you spend less than you earn you will have money left over which you can accumulate into building wealth. This doesn't mean you'll automatically have a fun and happy retirement, but you'll be stacking the odds of it in your favor.

If all these studies report that having a savings account will make you happy (or at least calmer), planning and saving for retirement should help make you feel happier along your journey. And if you think that living broke sucks, living broke in retirement will really suck!

Money Savings Worksheet

Do you actively look for ways to save money off of a purchase price?_____

How can you get better at buying only products and services you need or use?_____

Do you return items that you're not satisfied with or that you won't use?_____

If not, what are your reasons? How will you overcome those reasons?_____

How much do you feel you need in an emergency savings account?_____

Do you have an emergency savings account?_____

Does (or would) having a savings account make you feel happier or calmer?_____

Have you thought about how you would like to spend your retirement years?_____

What would you like to do after you retire from working fulltime?_____

How much will you need in combined assets and savings to live how you want in retirement?_____

Chapter #8

How much does it really cost?

*"But it's only pennies a day, you can afford that!"—Famous
words of a Salesmen*

It's expensive to be poor. Why? The obvious reason is that when you're poor you can't afford to buy very much, including food. But the biggest reason it's expensive to be poor is that everything in life will cost more and consume more of what little money you have. You will pay higher interest rates and you will have fewer options for getting loans or credit. You'll also pay more for certain services or have to pay up front for things. This means you'll have fewer options to buy services or shop for products. If you can't obtain credit cards or store credit cards then you're limited to shopping at places like Rent-A-Center if you need to make large purchases such as a refrigerator, stove, computer, furniture, etc. You'll end up paying double, triple, even quadruple what something would normally sell for. (These businesses offer a legal service to poor people so I'll refrain from saying what I think of such businesses.)

If you don't have a regular checking or savings account you'll have to cash your paycheck at a check cashing service and they'll charge you 5% for your own money. So if your paycheck is $300 you get $285 back. If you need to pay a bill by check (rent, medical, utility, etc.), you'll have to use a check writing service, and they'll charge you 5% for each check they write for you. If you need to send your landlord a $200 check it will cost you an extra $10. You're giving away money to access and use your own money. Without a regular checking account it will cost you up to 10% of what little you earn just to be poor.

When you are poor or broke everything costs more. Prices for products are still the same for everybody—a gallon of gas is the same price no matter your race, religion or financial status—but if you have a limited amount of money to spend, a gallon of gas costs a poor person more. With less money you have fewer choices and when you're broke you sometimes have to choose between buying gas for your car or toothpaste. I'm not joking. Even auto insurance, renters or homeowners insurance will be more expensive. One of the criteria that Insurers base their rates on is your credit score. If you have a low credit score you pay more. This doesn't seem fair, but there must be some historical basis for this. Or maybe it's simply because insurance companies can get away with charging poor people more?

When you're poor and have a low credit score, interest rates will be higher for everything, that's if you can get traditional financing or an auto loan. This is because people with low credit scores historically default more frequently on loans than someone with a good credit score. Those finance companies want to make up for those default losses and the smaller amount that they earn on lower interest rate loans given to people with higher scores. They do this by charging poor people astronomical interest rates. You personally may have paid every single one of your debts throughout your life, but if you have a low income or a high debt-to-income ratio, you'll have a low credit score and pay more for loans and many other services.

Other financial services offered to poor people are PayDay Loans, Cash-for-Title services, etc. The interest rates at these type of places are outrageous and the repayment terms are completely in THEIR favor. If you have a loan from one of these places you could go pay off your loan tomorrow, but you'll still be obligated to repay the FULL amount of interest. All this is legal and it's clearly stated in the terms of the agreement. The print may not be very large but the terms ARE there. The idea is to keep you in debt (to them), for as long as possible. It's unfair that those who can least afford to pay higher interest rates are virtually forced to pay the highest interest rates. But if you're poor or broke and need money, where else can you turn? That's the high cost of being poor or broke.

There's a difference between using credit and having credit available. You don't want to live on credit but you do want to have credit available if you need it. We all will likely need to use a line of credit at some point in our life; to buy a car, a home or some major appliance purchase. You need a credit card to stay at a hotel, rent a car, make plane reservations, etc. Credit and credit cards are part of our economic system and they are the only way you can make certain purchases. Poor people can get credit cards but they're not really "credit." Money must be deposited into the account first before the card can be used. And guess what? The credit card company is holding on to YOUR money and not paying you any interest. (At least a bank will pay you an insultingly low interest rate to hold your money.) Having credit available makes life a bit less stressful.

What can you do if you have a low income and low credit score and currently have few options for credit? If you don't have a traditional checking or savings account you won't be able to get a regular credit card or a store credit card. You seriously need to have a checking account with a national bank, local bank or credit union. There may be certain minimum balance requirements ($100) and you may have to wait up to 3 days before money can be accessed, but you will be able to cash your paychecks and write checks for free (usually). Any inconvenience of minimum balance or a hold on funds will easily be worth the savings in check cashing and check writing fees. And it will be the beginning of you establishing your good credit.

Once you have a regular checking account you'll then want to start reducing your debt and always pay your utility bills on time. You may not realize this, but it's very important towards your credit score to pay your utility bills on time, even if you're a high earner and already have credit cards. If you can't pay your gas or electric bill in full, call and make payment arrangements. They will allow you to pay what you can, but don't just ignore it. Talk with someone in the billing department and your call will be noted in your account. If you don't call, the utility company has no idea what's going on with your account and late or partial payments will automatically be recorded in your account and dramatically harm your credit score. Paying bills on time, even if it's just the minimums, will improve your credit score.

Once you have a good enough credit score to get a store card or traditional credit card, use it to make some small purchases, but make certain to PAY THE BALANCE IN FULL by the due date. This will show that you're credit worthy. Don't go crazy and charge a bunch of stuff and carry a balance. This will only show that you make payments, but it won't help your credit score or reduce your debt-to-income ratio. And if you won't have the money to pay the balance in full, then DON'T charge anything.

The high cost of Credit Cards: This is a cost many of us don't like to look at. If you charge $500 and only pay the minimum, that $500 will have an additional cost of about $200. Even if you pay off a $500 charge in 3 months you will have to pay back about $536. That's $36 you're paying to use someone else's money for a few months.

All *legitimate* loans (auto loans, mortgages, personal bank loans) and credit cards must give you a "Truth In Lending Statement." This document shows you—either right up front on the contract or on your monthly statements—just how much EXTRA you are paying. Many people don't want to look at that figure, they just want what they want when they want it.

Sometimes we need to use credit, sometimes it's good to use credit. Having credit available is like having a savings account; it gives you security. And the only way to establish credit is to have a credit history. You must have had loans in the past to prove your credit worthiness. The more credit you've had—and paid off on time—the better your credit score will be.

Paying off credit cards: If you're carrying a balance on your credit card, then everything new you charge will be added to your average daily balance. So that means you're paying interest tomorrow on what you bought today. So if you have a $2,000 balance and you charge up $100 more and then pay $100 plus the minimum payment (let's say a total of $140), you're still paying interest on your most recent charges. This is legal for credit card companies to do. So if you want to pay off your credit card debt, but still need to use a credit card for various purchases, then consider using this strategy: Consolidate all credit balances onto one credit card account and use a different card, that has a zero balance for current purchases, but make sure you pay that particular credit card balance in FULL every month when it's due.

I briefly touched on this in an earlier chapter. There are different strategies to paying off credit cards. Some say to pay the highest interest cards first. That makes sense, but you may be better off if you consolidate. If you can, transfer the highest interest balance to a lower interest card or loan. There is typically a 4% fee on balance transfers, but if you can go from a 24% interest rate to a 13% or 15% interest rate you'll be paying less in interest while you're paying off the debt. Here's how it works:

$3,000 at 24% interest over 3 years = $4,237.15 ($117.70 monthly)
$3,000 with 4% transfer fee = $3,120
$3,120 at 15% interest over 3 years = $3,893.61 ($108.16 monthly)

That's a $343.54 reduction in interest that you won't be paying. This may not sound like a lot of money, but when you're broke every penny counts. It's not uncommon for most people to be carrying a balance on 3 separate credit cards. If you can consolidate all of your credit card debt onto one lower interest card the savings really add up. However, you want to see a reduction in interest of at least 3% or the transfer fee won't be worth it. (Going from 18% interest to 13% is worth it.) Even if it isn't a huge savings in interest, credit card consolidation can get you to a zero balance on one or more of your credit cards. Then you can use the zero balance credit card for current purchases and pay no interest, providing you pay that card and those current charges off every month

Another strategy is to pay off the lowest balance first, no matter the interest rate, and pay only the minimum on the higher balances. Once you've completely paid off the lowest balance card you can use that one for current purchases, but be sure to pay the balance off every month. You could also pay off the lowest interest rate card and then transfer higher interest balances to that lower rate card. The main idea is to have at least one card with a zero balance and always pay off current charges on it. And if you're not going to have the money to pay off current charges, DON'T charge anything. Paying off debt is never painless, but once the debt is gone it's very freeing and calming.

The mathematical example I gave you above is based on the premise that you will pay off the debt in 3 years without adding any new charges. The words, **"Pay only the minimum"** in big bold print on your credit card statement is the legal con game credit card companies play on you. You're "minimum due" is only 2% of your average daily balance. Most people think that if they pay just the minimum due they'll eventually get their balance paid off. The truth is that you *might* get the balance paid off in 6 to 8 years, as long as you don't add any new charges. If your balance grows by $100 in current charges, your "minimum due" only goes up by $2. So instead of paying $40 minimum due you pay $42 minimum due. You'll never get out of debt that way—the balance will just keep getting bigger and the credit card company will just keep making even more money off of you. Living poor is expensive but living with credit card debt is even more expensive. Pay only the minimum due and you'll be living in debt for life—and that will really suck.

Trying to save money can cost you money:

Saving on expenses is great, but being cheap can cost more than money. More money is wasted through buying in bulk, buying discounted items you'll never use, interest charges, do-it-yourself projects and free items. Let's break each one of these money wasters down individually. Take your own behavior and history into consideration as you read.

Buying in bulk. I like shopping at big warehouse stores like Sam's Club, Costco and BJ's. You can find some really good bargains on products that you use on a regular basis. But because they sell in "bulk" I usually end up spending more money on a shopping trip than I should. If I need toilet paper, rice, coffee, butter and eggs, I can spend over $100 just for those few items. Sure, I may come home with 36 rolls of toilet paper, 10 pounds of rice, 6 pounds of coffee, 8 pounds of butter and 4 dozen eggs, but laying out all that cash in one shopping trip may not have been in my best interest.

Buying in large quantities makes sense if you have the money to spend, have the storage space, will eventually use the bulk supplies and the cost per unit is lower. Let's go over one single bulk purchase, a 36-Pack of toilet paper for example. I know that eventually I'll use all of the toilet paper so it won't go to waste (figuratively). Storage space is another concern. Toilet paper won't spoil so I can hide rolls wherever I find space, but I couldn't do that with 36 steaks or a dozen whole chickens. None the less, I put one fresh roll on the dispenser and I have to hide the other 35. The cost for this 36-pack is $23.52 with tax. Again, it will last for a while but that's a good amount of money out of my budget being spent right now. This means I'll have to forego buying something else I need or want if I'm going to stay within my spending budget on this week's shopping trip.

I do price comparisons and I saw that my local food store has the same brand of toilet paper on sale as a "Buy-one-get-one-free" offer. When I buy one 12-pack for $12 I get the second one for FREE. That's 24 rolls for $12.72 with tax. I also found a $1 off manufacturer coupon online. I printed 2 coupons so my toilet paper was only $10.72 (warehouse clubs don't accept coupons). So for buying fewer rolls, using a coupon and shopping at my local store, my cost per roll is .45 cents. Buying in bulk at the warehouse store my cost per roll would have been .65 cents each. So in this instance buying in bulk isn't less expensive. I'll have to buy toilet paper again sooner, but I have 12 fewer rolls to hide along with $12.80 left in my weekly budget to buy something else I need.

But what about bulk items that are less expensive per unit or per ounce? If you have the storage space and the product won't rot before you eat it or use it, then it's worth buying. But it's also worth studying your own consumption habits. I always asked my friend Jennifer why she would buy the little bag of potato chips for .99 cents when she could get 5 times as many potato chips for $3.49? She told me, "I don't have $3.49 as part of my food budget, but I do have .99 cents. And if I buy the big bag of chips I'll just eat them all in one sitting, or throw half of them out." I couldn't grasp this concept until I found myself throwing out bags of salad and half full jars of salad dressing. I thought that I was saving money by buying the larger bag of salad (less per ounce), but I don't eat a lot of salads. I would end up throwing out most of it and in 6 months my 72 ounce vat of salad dressings would turn fuzzy. By trying to be frugal I was costing myself more money in the long run. I'm cheap and I want to pay the least amount per ounce for any food item I buy. However, by studying my own salad consumption habit I now buy smaller bags of salad. I spend and waste less money even though I'm paying more per ounce.

If you can afford to tie up larger amounts of money on a single product type, the cost is lower per unit or per ounce and you have the storage space, then buying in bulk may work for you. But consider your own consumption habits before buying a giant 144 ounce can of beans. You may be wasting more money than you're saving when buying in bulk.

Buying the cheaper brand. I admit that I'm inherently cheap, but I've learned that buying the cheapest brand or product isn't always the way to go. Once again you must consider your own needs, budget, what the product is going to be used for and how often you plan on using it

Cheap paint and cheap tools are a great example of wasting money and time. I needed to paint a couple of rooms and I figured I would buy the cheaper priced paint to save money, but it took 3 coats to cover the old paint. So in my attempt to save money I ended up spending more money and time than I had planned. I'm also a tool nut and I've bought cheaper brands of tools only to end up going back to the store to buy the name brand tool. Bad experiences with a cheap product can sour you on the entire product category. I've purchased the cheaper version of technology gadgets only to have buttons break, it's incompatible with other products and programs or it has limited functions. Then I think, "Why does anybody buy this crap? It doesn't work." But after talking with a friend who bought the higher priced name brand version, and trying theirs, I found out that it did work and it's a cool product.

Buying a cheaper priced item, just because it's inexpensive, is similar to buying things with a coupon or discount simply because you have the coupon or discount. What have you saved if you buy something with a coupon but you'll never use it? Buying stuff just because the price is cheap—and it doesn't work very well or you'll never use it or you can't afford it—is a complete waste of your own money.

Let's not automatically confuse a cheaper price to mean low quality. Grocery store "house brands" and generics are often the same quality as the name brands but are less expensive. Last year's model, floor models, demos or display models are fine and usually carry the same warranty as the brand new in the box version. Certified pre-owned vehicles, reconditioned appliances and electronics often have the same warranty as brand new. Buying "used" isn't being cheap or financially foolish and buying used may be all you're able to afford.

There are times when buying the cheaper brand is a wiser choice. I mentioned tools. You don't need to buy the full chrome plated mechanics tool set if you just need an emergency tool kit for minor home repairs. Sometimes you need a specific tool for one or two uses, or you might need carpeting, furniture and bedding for a guest room that rarely gets used, that's when the cheaper brand will suffice. For instance, I have an old pickup truck that I use to haul mulch, lumber and garbage to the dump. It needed tires so the cheaper brand of tires work fine for my purposes. I rarely use the truck and it will rust away before the tires wear out. Why spend outrageous amounts of money on something that is temporary or infrequently used?

Do-It-Yourself projects. Auto parts stores, department stores and hardware stores love us Do-It-Yourselfers. Annually we buy millions of dollars worth of tools and supplies that we never use. The tools sit on the workbench and the supplies sit in the garage or in the shed. And we're notorious for not returning unused materials. If we do return an item we often see some other shiny toy to buy while we're there, or buy supplies for another project that we'll never get to doing. I'm not insulting or criticizing you, I'm talking about my own past do-it-yourself buying habits. But I've changed that habit.

A seasoned do-it-yourselfer will begin accumulating a cache of tools, paint, hardware, lumber and supplies. Spending a few moments after each project to store away extra supplies in a semi-organized fashion will pay you back on a future project. The main reason for do-it-yourself projects is to save money. Wouldn't it be nice to hear yourself saying, "There were some rotted boards on the deck, so I used hardware I already had and lumber that I saved when I tore down that old shed. Then I used the leftover stain and treated the entire deck and you can't see any of my repairs. It turned out perfect and I saved about $90 in lumber, hardware and stain." This project didn't cost you any new money. You kept yourself out of the hardware store where you may have been tempted to buy something unrelated to this project and you saved time by not having to drive to the hardware store. The time you saved can be spent relaxing on your repaired deck grilling steaks that you bought with the money you didn't spend on lumber and materials. When you can re-use and repurpose materials that you already have you are hitting the Zen of a do-it-yourselfer.

I have been a do-it-yourselfer for many years. The more projects I do the more I learn and am able to take on bigger projects and repairs. By doing so many projects, I've also learned to buy more supplies and materials than I need for a given project. But I keep everything I just bought in one area and make sure my receipt is handy. I buy more supplies than required because I don't want to be half way through a project only to discover that I need more screws, a 45 degree elbow instead of a 90 degree elbow, etc., and then have to go back to the hardware store. I only open what I'm going to use, and if I do open something, I open it neatly and keep the original packaging just in case I don't use it and will be returning it. When I'm finished with the project I return all of the unopened and unused materials and have it credited back to my charge card. I feel like I'm earning money when I get a credit back on my account. I'm also not giving the hardware store any more money than necessary. Hardware stores and auto supply stores make a nice juicy profit off do-it-yourselfers that don't return unused supplies or cores.

The smartest do-it-yourselfers know what they shouldn't attempt to do themselves. If you don't have the skills you may end up spending more money by having to hire someone to fix your repairs. If you don't have the proper tools you may endanger your safety. If you don't have a proper jack, jack stands and follow safety procedures, a simple oil and filter change on your car may cost you your life. If you don't know a lot about auto mechanics, replacing the brake pads on the family mini-van may cost **them** their life. Live electricity can be hazardous to your health, and if wired incorrectly or improper gauge is used it can start fires. If you aren't completely sure about what you're doing then don't take chances. Being frugal is not worth endangering you or your family's safety.

Most hardware and auto supply stores offer free "How to" seminars or have free instruction booklets. Attend some of these courses. Check YouTube for free videos. The more you learn about repairs and mechanical principles the better off you'll be. You may discover that you are fully capable of taking on certain projects. You may also discover that another project is too involved for your liking, but at least you'll have the knowledge of what needs to be done and the process of the project. You'll less likely be sold products, repairs and services that you don't need if you do end up hiring a contractor, repairman or take your car in for service.

Do-it-yourself projects can be fun, emotionally and financially rewarding. But if you don't have the skills or time to finish the project and do it correctly, you will be better off paying someone else. You're not just paying for someone else to do it, you're paying for the right to make sure it's done correctly. Remember that the smartest do-it-yourselfers know what they shouldn't do themselves.

Free items: Look at this incredible offer: *A new cell phone is FREE!* But it's only *free* if you sign a 2 year service contract, which is going to cost you at least $60 a month (with tax, FCC fee, etc.). That comes to $1,440 over 2 years. So the phone really isn't free is it? Plus, to get the most out of this new gadget you will want to add some extra services, apps, maybe buy music, ringtones, movies, eBooks, whatever. True, you'll receive a service and the use of a phone for your money, but the phone still **isn't free** and the gadget will probably end up costing you more than the stated contract price.

Your cost of time in learning and using the new device should also be taken into consideration. You may be better served (and spend less money), by getting a basic phone that you only just make phone calls with. Do you need text and web browsing ability? I don't care for texts. But sometimes texting does come in handy. I have the less expensive package where I get unlimited calling but only 50 free texts per month. All of the extra and unlimited services increase your monthly cost. Consider your style and usage before committing to a contract. Even a "pay-as-you-go" cell phone plan might be perfect if you don't use a cell phone much, or maybe start with a "pay-as-you-go" plan for the first few months and then determine what services suite you best and what amount of money you can afford to spend monthly.

Let's also consider the cost of what you COULDN'T purchase because your limited money has now been spent on this new phone contract, unless of course you just charge more stuff and services and further increase your debt load. That's what broke people do.

Even something as "harmless" as getting a **free** puppy or kitten will cost you money and time. That free puppy costs an "average" of $1,800 per year. Cats are a little less expensive but not always. Costs involved with this free puppy or kitten include food, vaccinations, toys, grooming, random vet visits, damage to home and belongings. You may not be able to take your dog or cat with you on vacations—so you have to pay for boarding. A dog may limit your entertainment or other commitment plans because you have to be home at certain times for feeding or to let them out. There's also the time in training and attention—that a dog is justly due—which takes time away from other activities.

This is NOT to say that you shouldn't get a dog or cat. (I have 4 dogs.) But there is a commitment and hidden costs in money and time to pet ownership. On the positive side you will likely get more exercise, that's if you walk your dog on a regular basis. If you really love your pet(s) you'll get companionship, enjoy their company and have opportunities to socialize with other pet owners. The time and attention which a dog requires can draw you away from other useless activities, like sitting and watching Reality TV shows for hours on end.

And then there's the "Try it now FREE for 30 days," or "The first 90 days is FREE then it's only $5 a month after that. You can cancel at any time and get a full refund." Very few people ever remember to cancel. It just becomes another line on your credit card statement buried among all the other purchases, month after month after month. A handful of those "Try it now" offers can add up to an additional $50 or more per month.

Some of you might be saying, "I never buy into those offers and I always check my statements and cancel recurring things I don't use." Be proud of yourself then—YOU are in the minuscule minority. I have friends who see the .99 cent per month charge for something they don't remember buying or know what it's for. "Aw hell, it's only .99 cents. My time is worth more than that." Your time is worth more than that—and so is your money. Ignore it and it adds up. A dollar is still a dollar. After 2 years of ignoring it, it becomes $24. One phone call and a few minutes is all it takes to cancel it.

I love **free** items, but just be aware that everything **free** will come with some costs. The costs may not be all that high, but there is a cost none the less. A free refrigerator from your neighbor will cost you money to run it. A free lawn mower may need some repairs. A free TV may cost you a disposal fee when it craps out in 3 months. The free cell phone requires a contract. Even with BOGO grocery store promotions you still have to **buy one** to get one free. Getting something for free, that you need or want, may be a genuine and outstanding bargain, but don't fool yourself—there will be a cost. All I'm asking you to do is to think whether the cost will be worth it to you because **there are hidden and added costs to *everything*.**

A car is a great example of this. (I'm not trying to insult you with the simplicity here—many of you already understand this concept.) A car requires costs involving regular maintenance, insurance, annual registration, parking or storage and of course fuel. The less you use the car the less you spend on fuel and parking. This also means you may spend less on maintenance like replacing tires, brakes and things that normally wear out with higher usage. But if you infrequently use the car it may cost you more in maintenance because the less you use a machine, and the longer it sits, things begin to rot, stick and break. Then the next time you start your car something's squeaking, rattling or falls off.

If you rarely drive your car and don't put many miles on it that means your insurance and annual registration will cost more *per mile driven*. If you pay $1,200 a year for auto insurance—it's the same price—regardless of whether you drive 6,000 miles or 36,000 miles a year. The more you drive, the lower your *cost per mile* on insurance and registration. But the more you drive the more you will spend on fuel and regular upkeep. Some insurers offer a lower rate based on miles driven. This means that you are covered for up to a specified amount of miles. If you drive fewer than 6,000 miles per year, ask your insurance company if they offer this type of policy. You may end up saving yourself a lot of money on insurance.

There are so many things we buy that come with hidden or added costs. Many of these things are items that we either never use or the item doesn't fulfill the vision of happiness we had when we were buying it (boat, pool, camper, snowmobile, golf clubs, hot tub, you name it). It isn't that salespeople are hiding costs from you; it's up to YOU to think beyond the purchase price. You're not just buying a boat, you WILL spend money on fuel, maintenance, docking or launch fees, storage and party supplies. If you finance purchases through loans or credit cards you'll pay interest, and that adds even more to the cost.

I'm certainly not saying that you shouldn't buy or finance products or toys. That choice is up to you, and if the item brings you joy and creates great experiences for you, then the cost may be worth it. My point is to show that most material items cost a lot more than what's reflected on the price tag. And not just the financial cost either. Time spent playing with "Toy A" means that you won't have time to spend with "Toy B," or worse yet, you may not have time to spend with the people you were hoping to entertain or enjoy the toy with. For most of us, everything we buy during our life equates to working more hours to pay for it.

None of this is intended to talk you out of buying things like a boat, camper, pool, TV, latest phone, pet, whatever. "Stuff" is fun to have and having the right stuff allows for you to have fun experiences. I just feel that it's important to understand that there are hidden and extra costs to *any* item. Think about how much something REALLY costs before you buy it or accept it for free. If you spend the time to think, you'll save a lot of money by NOT buying things you'll never use or by realizing that the cost is too high. There is a cost to everything and there's an especially high cost to being poor.

How much does it REALLY cost Worksheet

Do you pay off your current credit card debt every month?_____

Do you look closely at what you're paying in interest charges?_____

Do you have a tangible plan to reduce credit card and loan debt and what is that plan?_____

Do you pay utility, credit card and loan bills on time?_____

Do you automatically think that buying in bulk is cheaper?_____

Do you compare prices and equate the cost per unit or cost per ounce?_____

Do you buy things simply because you have a coupon, a discount or it's a cheap price?_____

Do you buy all sorts of materials for Do-It-Yourself projects and never complete the project?_____

Do you return unused materials after you complete a project?_____

Do you accept free products and jump at promotions because you see the word FREE?_____

Do you think about any additional or hidden costs before agreeing to something FREE?_____

Do you weigh out the stated and hidden costs before you commit?_____

Do you want to spend your entire life working just to pay off "stuff?_____

Do you want to spend the rest of your life poor, broke and in debt?_____

Chapter #9

Need-VS-Want.

"Do you NEED that or do you just WANT that?"

There is a profound and hope inspiring lyric in a classic Rolling Stones' song (paraphrased): "You can't always get what you want, but if you try sometimes you just might find, you get what you need." Well, as nice as this sounds, rarely do you ever get what you want and a lot of times you don't even get what you need. The truth is that you just get what you get and you have to make the best of it. That's what this chapter is about.

We all want to live comfortably, to enjoy the conveniences of modern-day technology and even have a few luxury items. There's nothing wrong with wanting nice things, that's what money is for. But there is a distinct difference between **needs** and **wants**, and sometimes they cross in the middle of one another. But don't veil a *want* as a *need*—be honest and clear with yourself about which is which. With a few examples and explanations I believe you'll be able to see the difference between the two.

We all **need** to eat, clothe ourselves and have someplace to live. You may **want** to dine at the fanciest of restaurants, you may **want** a giant house, you may **want** a brand new car every 2 years, and you may **want** the latest fashions and the coolest technology toys. But do you really **need** them? Are those things absolute necessities to sustain your life? They're nice wants and they're nice to have, but they aren't absolute needs. Life is expensive just the way it is and the more stuff you *want* the more expensive it becomes.

For instance you may need a car for work, for general transportation or to cruise around in and have fun, but the type of

155

car you want, and buy, may draw money away from paying for other more important needs. And when you do have a car it needs fuel, maintenance and insurance. Automobile ownership becomes more expensive than just the cost of the vehicle as we discussed in the previous chapter.

Depending on your career field you may have some unique needs that justify higher spending in some categories that wouldn't be essential for someone else. An attorney needs professional looking suites. Salesmen and office staff need proper business attire. A tradesman needs special tools or clothing unique to their craft. Your line of work may require that you're always available to be contacted and you need to have a cell phone or a smart phone with a variety of apps. Your health or a family member's health condition may require that you need a more comprehensive health insurance plan or special dietary needs. However, even under unique career and life conditions, wants are often veiled as needs.

And there certainly are many things that you **don't need**, yet advertisers, salesman and "conventional wisdom" say you should have it. You don't need auto insurance if you don't have a car. However, in most states you must have proof of minimum insurance levels to legally drive a car even if it's not yours. If your car is more than 6 years old you probably could get by with minimum coverages and the highest deductibles. You don't need a very large life insurance policy if you're single, but you might want to consider disability insurance. If you're married or have children you most certainly do need life insurance and disability insurance, but you don't need a multimillion dollar policy. Life and disability insurance will be discussed in the final chapter.

From my own experiences in life, I find that *wants* are more susceptible to rapid change than are *needs*. There is no question that needs can and do change rapidly. The loss of a job, an illness or death in your immediate family can change your needs. An unexpected pregnancy can change your needs. But most often, a divorce, marriage and building a family are planned (or somewhat planned) changes. There will be increases in needs at certain times

156

and at other times your needs will decrease. As your life conditions change your needs will change.

Wants on the other hand are influenced by whims, peers, advertising, geographical location, education level, social status, financial status, your personality and interests. Many financial decisions that people make are the result of desires and impulses (wants) instead of rational, calculated thinking and comparison (needs). This is not a criticism of humanity or an inference that people are gullible and easily influenced. I know that I can become obsessed with something and allow my wants to take precedence over my needs. I've developed a strategy that I use to overcome my impulses, which I'll describe shortly. But first I would like to give some evidence on my claim that many people make decisions based on wants instead of needs.

I learned more about human nature while selling cars than anywhere else. In most sales professions, we are trained to discover a customer's needs and then fill those needs. But people don't always make choices or purchases because they need something. But they will sell themselves on what they *want*. I sold a lot of cars and had a lot of referrals from satisfied customers because I would help people get them what they wanted. I didn't have to use slick car salesman tactics to get people to buy from me. Once I discovered what someone really wanted, I did whatever I could do (legally and ethically) to help them get the car they desired, even if I knew it wasn't their wisest choice. I told many a customer that a certain car was overpriced, outside of their needs or beyond their budget, but THEY wanted it. My job was to get them what they wanted, not to talk them out of something. My fellow salesmen and my bosses were a bit surprised by how well my method worked.

So the important question to ask yourself is: "Do I need this or do I just want this?" It's pretty easy to conjure up reasons for why you need something, so be brutally honest with yourself. Look, if you can afford it and it will make you happy then buy it. But remember that everything is an exchange. So even if you can afford something, there will be consequences that come with making the purchase. You may not be able to afford something else that you also want. You may have to adjust your needs because you just spent too much money on a want. The money you spent on a want may adversely affect the level of existence of those who you are responsible for.

However, you can use your wants and desires to propel you to accomplish more, work harder or be more frugal today so you can get what you want tomorrow. If you want a certain type of car or a certain house then you'll have to analyze and asses what you need to do to obtain it. Will you have to earn more, save more or sacrifice something else? Broke people don't do this, they just buy, buy, buy and then go buy some more. They have no self-control and take nothing into consideration or evaluate the ramifications of impulsive purchases, which are often veiled as needs. But the mathematics of wanton spending will eventually catch up with a broke person.

The 72-hour rule. This is the strategy I use to overcome my impulse to buy things on a whim or solely because I want it. I try to follow this rule with most purchases that aren't pure necessity (i.e. food, gas, medical care, etc.). I will go shopping, compare products, do my research, whatever is required, but I will hold back for 72 hours before making the purchase. Quite often during that time I will get a better idea of what I really need or want in the product I'm looking at. I may find a better deal or find a different product that suites my purpose better. A lot of times I won't even buy the product at all. After 72 hours I find that I can survive just fine without it. And I follow a "rule of thumb" dollar amount. Anything that's $50 or more, which isn't an obvious necessity, I try to wait 72 hours before I make the purchase.

I would like you to try the following experiment out on yourself. The next time you see something you want, take a piece of paper and write this out:

- What the item is.
- Where you'll get the money to pay for it and how you'll pay for it. (cash, check, credit?)
- How often or for how long you think you will use it.
- How or why you think having this item will enhance your life.

Place that sheet of paper prominently on the front of your refrigerator, then force yourself to wait 72 hours before you buy the item. On the fourth day take that sheet of paper, sit down and ponder over your list. Do you still want the item? Do you still think it will enhance your life in the same way as you had originally written? Have you survived just fine without it? Can you survive just fine without it? Have you found a better deal or an alternative that will serve your desires better? Or did some other shiny new toy grab your attention in the meantime, and now you don't even care about this one?

If you didn't buy this particular item, what will you do with the money you DIDN'T spend? If you had the money to buy it, will you put that money into savings or is that money burning a hole in your pocket? If you were planning on charging or financing the item, think about how much you just saved yourself for not buying it and pat yourself on the back. You will find that if you practice the 72-hour rule you'll end up saving yourself thousands of dollars over your lifetime. This is where procrastination can really pay off.

Think it out before you buy. You really really want the newest iPhone that you saw, and it's on sale for only $300. You already have a cell phone that suites your needs just fine, but you really want this cool new phone. Now, you could do what broke people do and go buy it on a credit card, commit to a 2-year service agreement and not consider how you're going to pay for all this. But you live by a budget and you have enough self-control and you're smart enough to take the time to figure out how you can make this happen. You know that this new iPhone is a *want* and it isn't something you absolutely *need* so you begin the process of doing the math.

Your current cell phone plan is $60 a month, which is already part of your budget, but the new iPhone service plan is going to cost $100 a month. You also realize that you will have to pay $300 for this new phone. (The actual cost of the phone will be $318 with 6% sales tax.) You don't have the $318 in your savings account so you decide that you'll put it on your credit card. You plan to pay the phone off over the next two years. (The real cost of the phone will come to $362.84 if you make 24 payments and your credit card charges 13% interest.) This will cost $15.12 per month and has to be added on to your budget. So with the cost of the phone and the extra $40 per month in carrier cost, this means you need to come up with an additional $55.12 more per month to pay for this. You know that your income is static and there's no way for you to earn the extra $55.12 a month, so you'll have to look at paring down or eliminating some other expenses currently in your budget.

As you go over your budget you determine that you can shave $20 off your monthly food allocation. This fancy new iPhone will have apps that get you more coupons and discounts so you won't be eating any less (that's what you tell yourself). You also determine that you can shave $10 off gasoline expense if you drive a little less and plan your trips and errands more efficiently and use one of the "Gas Buddy" apps. This new cell phone service plan has unlimited internet so you can cancel your internet service and that will save you another $15 a month. But your internet service is bundled with your cable (at $75 a month), and the "cable only" package will be $65 so you're really only saving $10. You call your cable provider and find out that you can switch to basic cable for only $43 a month, so you opt for that.

You've now shaved $62 off of your expenses and that covers the additional cost of your cool new iPhone. Plus you have about $7 a month extra, which you could send back to your food budget or sign up for Netflix internet only service because now you just have basic cable. That wasn't as painful and difficult as you thought it would be and you're still living within your budget.

This sounds like a lot of time consuming thinking, elements of self-control and planning doesn't it? Well that's what you need to do if you want to avoid living broke. Or you could just not think about it, charge the new phone, go deeper into credit card debt, commit to more monthly bills, then grumble and complain that you have no idea where all your money goes. That's how broke people live—but not you.

The difference between need and want with a job. We all want to work at a job that we love doing and get paid handsomely for doing it. Your mission is to find a job or career that falls somewhere within that spectrum. But that isn't always the case. Sometimes you have to work at a job you dislike and with people you don't care for. Your needs come first and earning a living to buy food, clothing and shelter are absolute needs. Earlier I talked about my job in auto sales. I hated that job! I hated the long hours, I didn't care for my bosses and I wasn't very close with my coworkers, but I loved interacting with customers. So I decided to make the best out of a miserable job. I spent more time chatting with prospective customers and less time kibitzing with my coworkers and I didn't hang out with my colleagues after work. I did quite well as a salesman and I made a lot of money for the dealership and myself. This was my proverbial "Golden Handcuffs," working at a high paying job that I hated.

I needed to earn a high income because I wanted to get myself out of debt and build a nest egg so I could pursue a different line of work. And that's exactly what I did. I worked for that car dealership until my debts were paid off and I felt I had enough in savings to ride out a career transition. That miserable job consumed 13 months of my life. But now I have a fulltime job that I actually enjoy. I eliminated my debt so I don't have the same level of pressure to earn as much as I once did. This affords me the luxury of spending more time doing writing. Writing is an avocation for me and not my main source of income. (This may surprise many of you but being a writer is not all that financially lucrative.)

Many people find themselves shackled to "Golden Handcuffs." They work at a high paying job that they hate because they also happen to live an expensive lifestyle or have a lot of bills to pay. My friend Bob (from Bob and Lisa in a previous chapter), is an example of this. Bob spent more than 10 years shackled to his "Golden Handcuffs" until his employer didn't need him any longer. Bob found himself in a financially uncomfortable situation but he also grew and learned a lot from it. Bob's story has some enlightening twists, some lessons for all of us and comes with a happy ending.

Bob and Lisa weren't living beyond their means, but because they did have a high income they purchased a lot of things they wanted and thus had a lot of bills. They owned a very nice home (with hefty monthly mortgage payments), 2 cars (with loan payments), and also had two children attending college which Bob and Lisa were paying the tuition. When Bob lost his job the entire family rallied. Their kids are reasonable and responsible and viewed this as a family problem, not just their parent's problem. One of their kids switched schools, where she received a grant and the other took on a student loan to complete his final year. This action by their kids really helped lighten Bob's financial responsibilities but Bob and Lisa still had big monthly commitments to pay and things still looked bleak.

To make their matters even worse, shortly after Bob lost his job Lisa also lost hers. This wasn't due to their own actions, the companies they worked for were restructuring. Fortunately Bob and Lisa had made some wise financial decisions a couple years before these unlucky occurrences happened. Home mortgage interest rates had tumbled to all-time lows so they refinanced their home. They had 22 years left on their mortgage but instead of getting another 30-year mortgage (along with some extra money as many people do), they converted to a 15-year mortgage. This maneuver kept their payments about the same but it took 7 years off of their future obligation.

Not only were they facing a lot of bills after their loss of incomes, their health insurance and other benefits were going to end. This posed even higher financial stress. Bob and Lisa needed jobs right now and they both wanted to find jobs they liked and that would pay the same as they had been previously earning. They both knew this wouldn't be as easy as it sounded. Bob had been earning over $100,000 a year and Lisa was earning $32,000 a year. As Bob told me, "There aren't a lot of $100,000 a year jobs floating around out there just waiting to be filled. You don't walk into a giant corporation, head into the CEO's office and ask, when can I start?"

Bob needed to earn an income, so while he was presenting his résumé to various large companies he took on a couple of part-time jobs. He worked during the day as a Security Guard for Ross retail stores and he was a general laborer glazing hams at The Ham Store in the evening. "Look, I needed an income and no job is below me, so I did what I had to do." He was offered a job in auto sales at a large car dealership. He wasn't looking for this position, but it would pay better than his two part-time jobs. All during this time he persevered and continued sending out his résumé and doing follow up calls. His persistence paid off. After 18 months of "belt tightening" and working at lower paying jobs he had an offer to work as an adjuster for a large Insurance company. Bob had never done this type of work but they were willing to train him.

After about 1 year of working as an adjuster, some of his superiors noticed Bob's extraordinary work ethic and his ability to fluently speak multiple languages. He was offered an elevated position where his talents would be better used. This resulted in higher pay, better job security and a chance to do work that he really enjoyed doing.

All during this time Lisa was busy as well. When they first became unemployed Lisa got busy by slashing and paring their budget. The first thing was to eliminate "luxury" expenses. She cancelled their premium cable package and switched to basic cable. She canceled their pool and lawn care services. Bob and Lisa would now do their own pool and yard work (together) on weekends. There was to be no more frivolous dining out and better use of food purchasing money. Every unnecessary expense was reviewed and either pared down or eliminated. Lisa found better deals on almost everything they needed and they both discovered that they could survive just fine with fewer luxuries. Lisa also eventually landed a job. It pays less than her previous position but she finds it to be fun and gratifying work for her.

Bob and Lisa certainly struggled for a while and there was some domestic stress between them. But the irony is that their inconvenient situation has ultimately brought them closer together. Bob and Lisa currently earn 35-40% less than at their highest income point, but their standard of living and enjoyment of life has improved. "We became wiser consumers. We changed the way we spend money and what we value. We learned how to make do with what we have. Mark, you know us personally and you can clearly see that we don't live in hardship or a substandard existence. We both have a better grasp of our financial needs and wants and we discuss our future more. I can honestly say that we have a higher appreciation for what we have and for each other."

What you want and what you need in relaxation and entertainment: This is an area of life that eats up a LOT of money. It's also very subjective to the individual. Your idea of entertainment and my idea will be very different. Some people want to go out on the town every night or every weekend. Some are happy to just sit quietly at home and unwind from their week of work. Some people feel they deserve a vacation every 6 months or every year and should experience luxurious accommodations or visit some far away location. Someone else may think that a week of tent camping once a year is perfect for them.

Most of this comes down to self-control and honest assessments of what you can afford. And once again we return to personal desires and tastes. I am in no position to tell YOU what you should do for entertainment or what type of experiences you should spend your money on. But I can tell you what I believe I did wrong when I was living broke.

I spent a good portion of my adult life as a drunk and a drug addict. My life was all about entertainment—I considered getting loaded as entertaining. Most, if not all of my discretionary money was spent on booze and drugs. I was always broke and always seemed to have $10 less than I needed. (These are both figurative statements. I didn't need booze or drugs and if I wouldn't have bought them I wouldn't have always been broke, needing $10 more than I had.) I feel my biggest crime was that I robbed myself of true entertainment, relaxation, vacations and experiences by spending my money and time on getting drunk.

There are a few suggestions I will pass along. I believe that you should have recreation, entertainment and vacations as part of your monthly budget. I know from my own experience that once you start to party the night away, money and how much you're spending isn't of concern. I have literally burned through and pissed through hundreds of dollars during a night of having a good time. I'm not lecturing on morals or temperance, I just want to illuminate facts about money. Boozing it up costs money, and once that money has been pissed away on booze (literally), it no longer exists—it's gone.

If you know that you have a tendency to overspend when you go out, and if you're heading out on the town or going to an event, leave your credit cards at home and bring ONLY your budgeted and allotted amount of cash with you. Drinks will be the costliest part of almost any event, outing or venue that you attend. I was a heavy drinker, so I know this to be true. A round of beers at a Major League baseball stadium will probably cost more than the price of your ticket. I no longer drink, so concerts, dining out, sporting events, you name it are affordable now. I have money available for food, souvenirs or other stuff while at events. I suggest limiting how much you drink at events. I don't care about your level of consumption, I'm trying to save you money.

If you don't have "vacation" or "recreation" as a budget category, how will you pay for those things? Most people just charge plane tickets, hotel reservations, whatever to their credit card and worry about paying it off later. When you have a budget, and the money has been saved up, you'll have a reference point of how much you can spend on your vacation or night out on the town. When you have future vacation plans in mind, you'll know how much you need to allocate, within your budget, so the money is available when vacation time comes around.

Look, I'm not trying to talk you out of enjoying yourself, attending events, having a drink or foregoing vacations. Most of us have only a limited amount of money that we can spend on entertainment. I want to help you learn ways to enjoy your money and get the most fun out of your money. Without a plan, a budget and some self-control, entertainment, vacations and relaxation will become a thing of your past. If you've never budgeted for entertainment and vacations, why not try it? Not only will it give you months of something to look forward to, you might find your next vacation to be genuinely relaxing, knowing that it's already been paid for and not something that's burying you deeper in debt.

Don't veil a want as a need. Having a budget helps you clarify the difference between **needs** and **wants**. There's nothing wrong with wanting something, just be clear about it. Wanting things and buying your wants are fine, just understand that everything is an exchange. You may be exchanging something you need for something you want.

Wants can be delayed, needs must often be met immediately. You need food but you can limit yourself to buying ground turkey even if you want filet mignon. You need clothing but you don't have to wrap yourself in designer fashion if you can't afford it. You also need to take care of your health but you don't need massages, spa days or any other personal luxuries if you can't afford them.

Your primary mission should be to pay your most important bills first and on time. These include: Mortgage or rent, utility bills, insurance, car payments, minimum payments on any credit cards. These are categories that will adversely affect your credit rating if you don't pay them on time and you need good credit to not live broke.

Your secondary mission is to be able to afford some of your wants. Controlling unnecessary, impulsive and frivolous expenses will move you closer to affording some of your wants. You have a limited amount of money to spend. Life is expensive and the more you want the more expensive it gets. I'm sorry if you want more stuff in your life but you can't afford it. It's a fact that most of us have a limited amount of money to spend. We all must make some choices and we all must forego some of our wants.

There are a lot of materialistic and personal things I want in life, but I have also found that there is a cost to getting the things I want. Some of those costs just aren't worth it to me. The exchanges that must be made are too resource consuming. My resources are limited, so I often have to choose between two wants or choose between a want and a need, either because of money, time, capabilities, whatever. My needs come first and it is my needs that keep me working. My wants keep me thinking creatively.

Writing down all of your expenses and putting them into a budget will help you see the difference between needs and wants. Take a look at your budget categories. Put a red star next to your absolute needs—those are the items you must have to survive—and put a blue star next to the items in your budget that you could still survive with if you didn't have them. "I could never live without my iPhone." Yes you could. You don't need an iPhone, cable TV, Netflix, tobacco or beer to sustain life. You may really like these things and they're important to you, but they are still wants and should be marked with a blue star.

As I mentioned in the beginning of this chapter, some needs and wants cross between one another. My job, and maybe yours, requires that I have a computer and internet service but I don't need the fanciest computer or the fastest internet service. A cell phone is helpful for my business but I don't need the latest version of iPhone with every imaginable app. These items may qualify as red star needs, but if I was in a different career field I would consider them as wants. And just because I claim that I need them for work doesn't mean I can't spend the least amount of money possible on them. So in my case, I consider these items as a 50-50 mix between need and want.

Once you've reviewed your budget and all the categories and marked them accordingly, then add up the total for all of the red star items and the blue star items. Look at the amount of **your money** being spent on your blue star wants. Is the total of your blue star items almost as much, or more than your red star total? Are each of those blue star items worth the cost in money and worth the cost of your time to earn the money to pay for it? Are some of those blue star items taking money away from red star items or other things you might want instead? If you're living broke, just scraping by or continuously going deeper into debt, then those blue star items are some of the expenses you can pare down or eliminate altogether. You personally must decide if what you want is worth it. Is having more stuff worth living broke, working more hours or working at a job you hate?

Remember that what you want, what you need and what you get will all be different. But why not have goals, use your budget to achieve those goals and make the best out of what you do get? With the right approach, the right attitude and a bit of self-control and effort, many times you actually get more than you want. It's happened to me and I'm sure it has happened to you as well. If your goal is to not live broke, then you'll need to control your impulse to buy everything you want.

Need-VS-Want Worksheet

Do you veil wants as needs?_____

Do you impulsively buy things simply because you want them?_____

Will you establish a 72-hour rule before buying inessential or superfluous items that you simply want?_____

What will be your "rule of thumb" dollar amount or criteria for your 72-hour rule?_____

Have you at least tried the 72-hour rule experiment once?_____

How did the experiment work for you?_____

Do you understand that you may not always, if ever, get what you want or need?_____

Are you willing to make do with what you get? How?_____

Have you reviewed your budget expense categories and items to see which are genuine needs and which are wants?_____

Is everything you want worth the cost?_____

Chapter #10

What money *can* and *can't* buy.

"You're right, money can't buy everything. But it can buy most things."

In earlier chapters we looked at whether saving money—amassing it into an account or getting a reduction in price—makes people happy. We briefly touched on the subject of The Golden Handcuffs—working at a job you hate but pays you well—so you can buy lots of toys. (Some marriages are like this.) We talked about how costly carrying useless debt is and how expensive it is to be poor—both of which cause stress. I attempted to get you thinking about the difference between your needs and your wants and if the price to be paid is worth it. So here we're going to consider whether money can buy you happiness and further break down what money can and can't buy.

I agree that money doesn't buy everything, but without it you can't buy anything, unless you barter, which I'll touch on later. The purpose behind having money is so that you can afford nice things, live comfortably and be happy, right? But the vigorous *pursuit of money* can actually bring about emotional unease and undesirable behavior; greed, worry, unhealthy diet, theft, compromising morals, etc. The *lack of money* can also bring about emotional unease and undesirable behavior; fear, worry, unhealthy diet, poor living conditions, theft, compromising morals, etc. If money can elicit so many and similar emotions and behaviors in a person then we must ask: "Can money buy you happiness?"

There have been numerous behavioral studies done to conclude how much money someone needs to be happy. (I won't cite all the studies here or who did them because that's not the important part. If you're curious you can do a Google search with a few key words and you'll find the articles and studies.) It has been noted in these studies that after a certain level of wealth, people don't become exponentially happier as their wealth or income grows. In most of these studies an individual's level of happiness is based upon annual income—not on how much they have in savings, their amount of assets or their net worth. The studies don't state what level of debt these people have or what happens to the individual's happiness if or when their income falls or when they eliminate debt. The studies also don't explain **why** a person is happy at this income level. I'd like to break this all down a bit here.

For instance, these studies say that a person who earns $1,000,000 a year is not all that much happier than a person who earns $100,000 per year. The studies claim that after a certain level of money you don't grow happier. I beg to differ on this. I'm certain that someone who earns $1,000,000 annually (and has grown accustomed to it), wouldn't be very happy if their income dropped to $100,000 a year. They may be able to survive fine, but then again maybe not. Maybe their debt load and obligations are still based on a million dollar income. They now face financial stress and might even *feel* like they're poor. (Stop laughing, I'm going to be making a point here.)

Research from these studies shows that the average American becomes "happy" when they have an annual income of about $75,000 (that's at the time of this writing in 2015). Yet this figure of $75,000 is highly subjective. Do you think Paris Hilton would be happy with a $75,000 a year income? I highly doubt it. Depending on your level of debt, responsibilities, obligations, spending habits, hobbies, interests, tastes, style of living, geographical location and more, determines whether $75,000 is enough or not.

Studies like this can be pieces of interest and curiosity, but they don't reflect YOUR reality. At best they can give you a reference figure or give you goals to shoot for. At worst they can mislead you into thinking that you're doing worse than you actually are. If you have minimal obligations (no children, no mortgage, no auto loans, low debt), you may not need anywhere near an annual

172

income of $75,000 to be happy. But if you have a large family, large house, huge mortgage, auto loans, student loans, tuition and high debt, then even $75,000 may not be enough to pay all those bills and you'll have stress. Stress doesn't make very many people feel happy.

Further, even if your take-home pay is $75,000 a year but you spend every penny of it without putting anything into savings or towards your future, you're still living paycheck-to-paycheck, broke at the end of a pay period and may not be at ease. But if spending every penny you earn does genuinely make you happy, who is to say your lifestyle is wrong?

Averages and studies that reference a specific amount of money someone needs to bring them happiness are too subjective. The example of a multimillionaire winning $20,000 in the state lottery makes this point. An additional $20,000 to a multimillionaire is nice, but not as life changing as it might be for someone who is poor or flat broke. And I highly doubt whether someone who earns $74,995 would say, "I'm $5 away from being happy. But until then I'm unhappy."

So we return to the question: "Can money buy happiness?" I do know that money can buy *unhappiness*. Having money can bring out feelings of nervousness, worry, mistrust and suspicion of others. If you're always worried about earning more money, nervous about losing money, or are distrustful of people's intentions, then having money isn't fun—even when you do have plenty of money. Money has a way of changing how others see you and treat you. Some will envy you, some will despise you and some will pursue fake friendships to get at your money. Money can also change the way you see yourself and others. More money can buy you more stuff, but with that stuff can come more debt and more anxiety. So money doesn't buy everything, including happiness.

My belief is that what money **can buy** is mental security and peace. When you **don't** have enough money or must scramble monthly, weekly or daily to cover your debts and obligations you have anxiety and unease. When you **do** have enough money, either as income or in savings, to cover your debts and obligations then you will be mentally at ease. You will have a psychological state of calm. Mental calmness and ease can come when you don't have the anxiety of financial stress, the gnawing uncertainty of "how will I survive?" But that still doesn't guarantee that you'll feel happy or behave like a happy person. Genuine happiness is something you must foster within yourself and even poor and low income people are capable of that. Happiness is a state of mind, not necessarily more money or more stuff.

I have lived poor and broke and I didn't like it. I no longer live broke but I'm certainly not wealthy (that's by my own standards and Paris Hilton's), but I feel happy. I have more than I need but less than I want. This allows me to be happy. I'm not giddy and bubbling over with joy, but I am genuinely a happy person. Even after I rid myself of debt and could afford to live better it took me a few years to understand how to feel happy. I learned that if I fixate on earning more and pursue money too hard I can become unhappy. Even now I must consciously remind myself that I can and should be happy. There's no question that if I earned more money it would allow me to buy more stuff, but I don't really need more stuff, what I need is more of what makes me happy. But here's the weird twist; having more money available can help me get more of what makes me happy. Let me explain by involving you with some questions and thoughts to consider.

Which do you value most: Time? Health? Relationships and friendships? Self-actualization? Recreation? Creativity? Material possessions? Freedom? The weird twist is that it truly does require money to have any of these. Your age and how much of any of these you want will establish how much money you'll need. Let's go over each of these subjects.

Time: People who earn the most money tend to spend more time working. True, they can afford nice things and luxurious vacations, but enjoying their toys or going on vacation requires time away from work. Because they spend so much of their time working they don't have much time available for other activities. When they do go on vacation they might try to cram everything into a very tight schedule or they're constantly making calls, checking email or texting. They return home and go back to work worn-out from their vacation. Have you ever had a *vacation* like that? Do you have toys you never get to enjoy because most of your time is spent shackled to golden handcuffs?

As recent as 50 years ago most people actually spent MORE time working than relaxing than we do now, yet many talk about "the good old days when life was easier and a slower pace." Life wasn't easier, many jobs and household chores required tough physical labor. Today we have labor-saving and time-saving appliances and machinery. But with that machinery and technology comes time consumption. TV viewing requires time. Social media requires time. Look at how much time you spend behind the wheel of a car going to all the entertainment and shopping options you now have. Multitasking, like talking on a cellphone while driving sounds like a timesaver, but it's time consuming and mentally taxing. Pay scales and labor laws may mean we spend fewer hours at our job and many of our new technologies may be labor-saving, but all of these advances and innovations haven't given humanity any more time.

One hour is still the same duration today as it was 20, 50, 100 years ago. With all the advances in technology, in transportation and in living conditions we now have many more choices, which makes that one hour *seem* shorter. You often hear people say, "I just don't have the time to get everything done." Having all of these multiple options is what creates the feeling of living at a fast pace and not having any time.

There are actions, and inactions, you can undertake to make it *feel* as if you do have more time. Instead of multitasking try

175

singletasking. Consciously focus on doing one task at a time. Sure, you can be doing laundry while you vacuum with your iPod on. But if you start too many projects or try doing too many things at once you'll be bouncing around between projects and forget about something or have to stop what you're doing to go finish the other project. I have learned that if I focus on one task, complete it and then go on to the next, my work efforts are more efficient, I get more done in less time and the task is done properly. Then I can genuinely relax or go do something else that's more enjoyable. Singletasking makes me *feel* as if I have more time.

Walk slower. You will likely notice things—things which have always been there—for the very first time. Force yourself to slow down during meals or while engaged in intimate conversations. Turn your cell phone, iPhone, Blackberry or computer OFF once in a while. When you turn it back on you may discover that you didn't miss out on very much. At first some of these things can make you feel antsy, but you'll get used to it and it may change your entire perspective on how you want to spend your time and live your life.

Some people like a hectic schedule, thrive on pressure and always want to be connected. If that's you, then revel in the pressure, but please don't complain that you haven't enough time to relax or to enjoy simple pleasures in life. I like a hectic schedule and high pressure while I'm working at my job, but I absolutely do turn my job "off" when I'm done. After my workday is over I slow down my pace and want to genuinely relax and enjoy the fruits of my labors.

If you have more money you can pay other people to do some of your work, but then you have to exchange more of your time at a paying job to afford those services. Conversely, you **can't** pay someone else to serve as "you" when it comes to spending time with people you care about. I've been saying all along that everything is an exchange. Sometimes you have to exchange or forego an option so you'll have more time to yourself, to spend with people you care about or to live at a slower pace. Money can't buy you more time, but it can buy you more options of things to do with your time. Make the best of those options and enjoy your time in ways that are valuable to you.

Health: With money you can buy better health, but only up to a certain point. Money allows you to buy better food, pay for the best medical services, pay for the best gym memberships. Yet each one of these still requires your active participation. If you overeat and don't go the gym, even the best medical services won't help you. Following a healthy eating plan requires some dietary knowledge, time to shop for and prepare proper meals. Organic foods cost more. Gym memberships and personal trainers cost money. Clothing and home gym equipment cost money.

Your genetics, physical capabilities, eating, drinking and smoking habits all make a difference in your health. For instance, I drank heavily, used recreational drugs and worked out at a gym 5 days a week, but I still wasn't healthy. I was strong, yet I still had hypertension issues, headaches, hangovers, didn't have much physical stamina and carried some booze flab. When I eliminated destructive consumption from my life, the exact same exercises and exact same workout schedule made a dramatic difference in my strength, stamina and overall health. It took me no more time at the gym and no more money to improve my physical health. In fact I spent less money and became more productive at work and in life due to my improved health.

Your desire to have good health will require some self-control, physical effort and a commitment of your time. You don't need to be rich to eat healthy and exercise. No matter how much money you have, you can't pay someone else to lose weight for you or exercise for you. Money gives you more opportunities for good health, but YOU still need to participate in your own wellbeing.

Relationships: Money can buy you relationships and friendships. Some of those relationships and friendships may be hollow and last only as long as your money lasts. However, some friendships and relationships may last a lifetime. But money does have a way of changing the dynamics of things.

People of the same financial status seem to gravitate towards each other. When there are vast differences in status it can create awkward rapport between people, even among longstanding friendships. If you happen to be well off you might notice some of your friends and relatives, who aren't as well off, leaning on you for loans or financial assistance. This isn't always the case, but I'm sure you've heard, "I don't have the money to give you. Why don't you go ask your rich uncle? He has more money than he knows what to do with." It may be **you** who is (figuratively) considered the rich uncle. I'm not saying that people are money-grubbers, but if you do show any signs of wealth, someone at some time will ask for financial aid from you. If you have plenty of money and you want to be benevolent or share it with friends, that's up to you.

What I believe to be essential to your happiness is that you don't develop a sense of self-importance and use your wealth as leverage against those less fortunate than you. Don't feel that you are above others who are not in your financial class. Feeling grateful for your own financial condition can help make you a more humble and pleasant person. Just because you have more money than someone else doesn't make you a better person—it just means you have more money.

Most marriages are based on a "value" paradigm. Not many people like to look at marriage as a value exchange, but it's true. You must bring something of value to a marriage and enhance your spouse's existence, otherwise why would they want to invest their life with you? And you want your spouse to bring value and enhancement to you. This doesn't mean that the institution of marriage is legal prostitution or should be a cold business arrangement. But it only makes sense that you want to be with someone who helps to make your life better in some way. The value your spouse brings may be companionship, conversation, laughter, sexual intimacy, intellectual intimacy, money or all of these things. What you bring to one another doesn't have to be the same thing. Your arrangement may be that you are the breadwinner and your spouse brings something of value other than money. Marriage is teamwork with an exchange of value and services between the two participants which can't always be measured by a mathematical equation.

Failed marriages are the result of incompatibility and at the root of the incompatibility is either money or sex. If you and your spouse have dramatically different values and views on money, that money conflict can worm its way into every other area of your marriage, including sexual intimacy. When both you and your spouse hold the same or similar opinion on money there will be less conflict and tension between you.

Some marriages are based upon money. The participants are both bringing something of value to the relationship—one brings money and the other brings something else of value. Both parties are often well aware of the exchanges being made, but don't necessarily discuss it out loud. That doesn't mean it's a bad marriage, an unhappy marriage or is destined to fail. It's called "a marriage of convenience" and it may be a perfect arrangement for each person.

So yes, money can buy you friends, spouses, lovers and relationships. Is this comparable to prostitution? Maybe. But if you're getting something out of the exchange, and you feel the money is worth spending, then who's to say it's wrong? Just be aware that if or when the money runs out, some of those relationships will come to a screeching halt.

Self-actualization: Some people value self-actualization over money. The old saying of "Do what you love and you'll earn millions" doesn't always hold true. If you love walking dogs or crafting cute beaded jewelry you probably won't make millions, but you might earn enough to pay your bills and survive. Many people run their own small business for this reason. Sure they would like to be wealthy and have a high income, but they will exchange wealth and income so that they can do something they enjoy and that they feel is making a positive difference in other people's lives.

In my case, I love writing and I do hope to someday earn a living with my books, podcasts and website. But I prefer to stay self-published. I personally pay for every aspect of my books; editing, design, printing, distribution, shipping, marketing, advertising. Some of my projects have been money losing propositions and some things I give away for free. The reason I stay self-published is because I know that as soon as someone else says, "I'll pay you to write and let us publish your work,'" that it will then become a *job* to me. I'll have someone else setting my deadlines and demanding certain styles and levels of production output. I'll begin hating what I once loved.

That's why I still have a regular fulltime job where I earn my income for living. I do happen to enjoy most aspects of my job and I do feel rewarded emotionally. But it's still a job. I know that I am exchanging my time and talent for money and I don't mind having fleeting moments when I hate my job. My fulltime job does allow me time during the day to do some writing, but if I'm writing I'm not earning. My self-actualization through writing is important enough to me that I'm willing to forego some earnings.

Self-actualization is also why retirees or wealthy people provide their talents and services to charitable organizations. They feel they've earned as much as they need and want to actively do something philanthropic for humanity and not just donate money. The act of being involved in something benevolent gives them joy and a feeling of purpose.

Recreation: Some people value a life of leisure, travel or participating in a sport over money. Under the subject of recreation I'm also going to include entertainment. Entertainment may be dining out, movies, concerts, public sporting events, going to clubs or bars and alcohol consumption. Just about any type of entertainment and recreation will cost money and without having the time available, recreation is impossible.

For most of us, recreation is a reward for exchanging our time and labor at a paying job. The more time you spend at recreation the less time you'll have to earn money. Money is the limiting factor with recreation. You might say, "I have plenty of money, I just don't have the time." The answer to that problem is pretty simple—just quit your job and you'll have plenty of time to go golfing. But without a job you'll quickly run out of money to pay for your recreation. It's easier to come up with time for recreation than it is the money. For instance you would like box seats at a MLB game but all you can afford is bleacher seats. You want to go to Aruba but all you can afford is a weekend at a local beach. You may have the time for these activities, but without money the recreation is impossible.

Another big (if not biggest), expense under the heading of recreation is alcohol and drugs. The actual cost of the product(s) are high but the consequential costs of lower work production, higher frequency of illnesses and potential legal costs are incalculable. Even if you're not a daily drinker or user, alcohol at restaurants and clubs is expensive. Just go out to dinner one time and DON'T order any drinks. You'll be shocked at your bill. Again, I'm not preaching any moral or temperance stance. I just happen to know—from personal experience—that when drinking and/or drugs are part of your recreation routine, a lot of money is literally pissed away.

There's nothing wrong with buying recreation to reward yourself for your labors, that's what money is for. But if you don't want to live broke, then you seriously need to assess how much money and time you have available for it. Recreation is an item that should be part of your budget. Knowing how much money you have available for recreation (even if it's not a lot), will help you focus in on your choices and allow you to make better decisions to get the most out of your recreation dollars. Money can buy you more recreation and better recreation opportunities, but it still requires time to genuinely enjoy recreation.

Creativity: Some people are excited and driven by the challenge and experience of being creative. Employers in certain industries know that creativity is more important to workers than money. Companies like Google pay their employees well, however, they not only give their employees opportunity to be creative, they nurture it and make it part of an employee's work schedule. This type of work atmosphere draws some of the sharpest minds to Google.

But not every job allows for creativity. Some occupations and many jobs are repetitive tasks. A lot of people are willing to work at a good paying job—which is boring or they hate—just so they can afford to spend money and time on their own creative interests. Even for people who say, "I'm not very creative," there is certainly something they do that has their own unique thumbprint on it.

I believe that creativity also includes raising children—which costs money. A poor or low income parent must challenge their creativity to come up with ways to educate and entertain their children. Discovering, nurturing and bringing out a child's strengths calls for creativity. Helping a child grow into a happy, well-balanced adult challenges any parent's creativity.

Developing and living within a budget calls on your creativity. Getting the most distance and utility out of what money you have calls on creativity. Living within your means isn't all about sacrifice, it's about creativity.

Money doesn't make you more creative, but it does allow for more funds available so you can attempt at and play with a wider variety of creative undertakings. Being poor or broke calls on a different type of creativity. Use your unique mind to creatively move from living broke to living comfortably.

Material possessions: Some people like having lots of toys and flashy things. Some people just enjoy the act of shopping. It's clear that material possessions cost money. If you can easily afford buying material possessions and still meet your required bills, how wonderful for you. But most of us have a limited amount of money to spend, so we must make choices. Those who don't control spending or make impulsive buying choices generally end up living broke and in debt. Some people actually use debt as a way to motivate them to work harder. I would suggest against it, but if that's your method who's to say your wrong?

There's an old saying, (often displayed on bumper stickers or cute little placards in guys garages), "He who dies with the most toys wins." But what do you win? If it wins you happiness during your life that's wonderful. If it wins you envy and jealousy from your friends is that winning anything? Maybe it just wins you more debt?

Money can clearly afford you more material possessions, but more stuff may not make you any happier. Buying the right stuff—which enables you to have fun experiences—is what can make you happy.

Freedom: Money can buy you freedom—the freedom of choices. Money allows for the freedom to travel, to work or not work, to live where you desire and buy the things you want. But money can also become your slave master. Any addict will tell you that they feel like a slave to their substance and would like to be free from its grasp. Money, and what money buys, can become addicting.

I believe that religious and spiritual pursuits fall under the subject of freedom. Some people want to shed the shackles of money and material possessions to freely live a life of spirituality. But even then the individual needs at least some money to pay for food, clothing and housing, unless someone else donates or spends their money and gives them food, clothing and housing. Monks may be a self-sufficient group, but I don't think many Monks will be reading this book.

Money might be considered a necessary evil—because we all need some of it to survive. But money can buy you freedom, even if it's freedom with restrictions and limited boundary lines.

Regardless of what *you* value, we're all faced with the same dilemma: Without money you can't always enjoy your time, health, relationships and friendships, seek self-actualization, participate in recreation, experiment with creativity, buy material possessions and generally be free. A human's driving force is the pursuit of happiness. What you and I consider as "happiness" may be vastly different and what makes you feel happy today may not be the same in a day, a week, a year or 5 years. Will money alone make you happy? Probably not. But money can help get you more of and closer to the things that do make you happy.

Is chasing wealth dangerous?

My opinion is that chasing *anything* with disregard for who or what gets trampled in the way is dangerous. However, we return to some questions. How much money is wealth and what is wealth to you? What do you consider as dangerous? Some people would flounder along in life if they weren't chasing something (a degree, a certain car, a certain home, a certain person). Without a specific goal they don't go into chase mode. What is considered as an obsessive, unhealthy chase by one is another's normal accomplishment process.

Like most of the other questions and positions I present, the question of: "Is chasing wealth dangerous?" is completely subjective to the individual. I know that for me, I can become too overly focused on pursuing wealth and income. I become fixated by it and I stop having fun. Not just the fun of life which occurs after the work day is done but the fun of creativity and activity while working at earning the income. I lose perspective of enjoying what I currently have and can currently afford to do. I can even become depressed or pressured. I become distracted away from other things, projects or people that I should and I would like to pay attention to.

Chasing wealth and acquiring it can be fun. But just like an alcoholic, when drinking becomes a destructive addiction it isn't fun anymore.

What money CAN buy:

Many economists and psychologists like to say that "material items are just things and they won't bring you happiness." I disagree. Stuff can bring you happiness as long as the item enables you to have enjoyable life experiences. I do agree that the accumulation of stuff itself—as a result of peer pressure or advertising influence—may not bring happiness. But for some people the act of shopping and spending money is more enjoyable than the use of or the utility of the item purchased.

Life experiences are more memorable than products. Many studies have been done to show that there is less "buyer's remorse" when spending money on experiences than on products. Few people say, "I really should have bought that home entertainment center instead of going on that trip to Paris." Many people will regret (or feel like they regret), the purchase of an **item**. This happens because a similar item to the one you just purchased goes on sale, or there's a new and improved version, or the product doesn't perform as you hoped or imagined it would, it doesn't bring you as much joy as you imagined it would or you discover that you really didn't need it.

But products **can enable** for life experiences. Years ago I bought a pontoon boat and it has allowed for many great experiences with family and friends. I more recently bought a specific style of car because it enables great experiences. It's a very sleek and fast convertible. I know that it wasn't a financially wise purchase, I could have bought a basic car. But even when I go grocery shopping I get a lot of joy out of driving my little roadster. So for me the high cost was worth it. But I've also bought a lot of products that I thought would make me happy but they did nothing to enhance my life or enable for experiences. Those type of items were a complete waste of my money.

My point here is to get you thinking deeper about the things you plan on buying. If the item will bring you great experiences and joy, then buy it if you can afford it. But really think out the purchase—use the 72-hour rule (if not longer). The things that you buy, use and then have great experiences with, will create wonderful memories for you. But seriously think about the purchase, because regardless of whether you enjoy it or not, can afford it or not, once you own it, **parting with "your stuff" can be emotionally difficult and costly**.

I have had a hard time getting rid of some of my stuff for various reasons. Primarily I don't like to take a financial loss selling something for less than I paid for it. But most of the time I didn't sell or get rid of something because I was either emotionally attached to the item or I felt as if I've spent so much money and time on it that I can't get rid of it. Behavioral economists use various terms for these emotions: Sunk cost delusion, Endowment delusion, Entitlement delusion. These terms mean that what you purchased or created *feels* more valuable to you than it would to someone else.

Here's a real simple example. Let's say that back when you were in college you went to Key West with your buddies on spring break and you purchased a painting of two Tarpon playing pool for $50 at a street Artist fair. Years have passed and you still have it. It's a pretty good painting with a nice frame and (you think) it looks cool in your apartment, yet the painting serves no actual utility. But now you're moving in with your girlfriend, ooh and the painting of those wacky pool playing Tarpons doesn't match with her décor. She doesn't want "that thing" in her apartment so you figure you'll sell it at a garage sale, along with your mini Mr. Beer refrigerator and the singing bass. No big deal, you love your girlfriend and after all it's just stuff. But the price you're willing to sell these prized possessions for will likely be higher than what someone else is willing to pay for them. Why? Because they're *yours* and you have memories and emotional ties to the stuff.

Let me give you an example from my own life and then think if there was ever something similar in your life. I told you about the pontoon boat I bought. I spent a fair amount of money to buy a brand new pontoon boat. Over the years I had invested a lot of money and time taking good care of the boat (cleaning, repairs, maintenance, fuel). But those are sunk costs of money and time that can never be recaptured.

I did get plenty of use and enjoyment from having the boat. I had a lot of wonderful times entertaining on it and it's loaded with memories. But my life had changed and I no longer used it. It was more of a burden to winterize and store it than it was to keep it so I decided to sell it. But it was still "my boat" and I wanted fair market value for it (if not more). But no matter how much I wanted for it I would only get what someone else was willing to pay for it. It held no memories for them, so they only looked at the actual value of the boat, how much they would use it or wanted it, and naturally every potential buyer was looking for a bargain price.

I ended up selling the boat for less than I thought it was worth. Interestingly, once it was sold I didn't miss it. In truth I was relieved because I didn't have to deal with getting it ready for winter storage. I still have the memories. The physical boat doesn't hold the memories, my mind holds the memories and looking at pictures refreshes those memories. (A camera is another example of a "thing" that facilitates the experience of memories.)

Houses, cars, boats, campers, golf clubs, any inanimate item that brought you joy or you've spent time and money on plays with your emotions when it comes time to sell it. You fall prey to the sunk cost delusion. It's tough to sell things that have high memory value to you but low value to a buyer. You might even decide to not sell it because of memories or sunk costs, thus sinking even more time and money into it. Or worse yet, it rots away or becomes completely worthless due to neglect.

We all spend money on "things." By taking the time to think before you make a large purchase you may find that you'll be spending less money on useless items, and buying more items that enable for great experiences and create fantastic memories. You'll then be getting the highest utility out of your money. And that's the purpose of money, to live well and have great experiences.

Bartering your services:

I talked about the barter system earlier in the history of money. Well the system is still alive and thriving today, only on a different scale. In principle you barter your time and talents for a paycheck which gets you money and allows you to buy things, but you can barter your services for things that money can't buy. You can barter your time, talents and friendship to help out your neighbors, friends and organizations. What you get back in return may be more valuable than money.

I barter my mechanical and construction skills with my neighbors. This isn't a cold calculated business deal, but it reaps many rewards. I help them save money on projects and in turn they help me with some of my projects or do favors for me while I'm away traveling. The best part is that it builds friendships and sense of community between me and my neighbors.

It may sound "cold" to call helping a neighbor out a barter, but that's what it is. You invite friends over for dinner and typically they reciprocate. You help your buddy move and he'll most likely do the same for you. I don't expect anything in return when helping a neighbor, but often some type of gratitude is shown back to me. Neighbors and organizations that I've helped have hooked me up with friends of theirs who have given me money saving deals on windows, construction work, vehicles and more. (Some people call this "networking," but it's still bartering.) And as I said, the best part of the barter is in the building of friendships.

You can also barter your services to receive discounts off certain things. I know people who receive a discount off their rent because they vacuum and clean the apartment building's hallways once a week. Look for opportunities like this to get discounts. Offer to shovel or do minor lawn maintenance. People all around the country function as "work campers." They barter their time to clean and maintain a campground and they receive free camping or parking for their RV. I'll grant that you can't go on vacation, stay at a Radisson hotel and offer to vacuum the hallway in exchange for a reduced room rate, but there are things you can barter for to save yourself from spending money.

Construction workers, repairmen and computer nerds often use the barter system to get their counterparts to take care of something they can't do. An auto repairman may know nothing about computers, but his computer buddy does, so the two will swap services. A roofer will ask a plumber to swap services. The barter system is older than prostitution. (I'm not advocating prostitution, but it's an example). You can barter goods as well as services. You might have something you no longer use and your neighbor has something they no longer use. I have traded trailers, tools, snowmobiles, electronics equipment and musical instruments—things I no longer used or needed—for something I wanted or needed. No cash was ever exchanged in these barter transactions.

You have to think creatively, be willing to do some work and ask for the opportunity to barter. You have to think about your own skills and what you have to offer to someone else. Bartering can help you spend less money, conserving your cash for other uses. But the best part of bartering is that it can build friendships and open networking doors.

Money itself can't buy happiness, but with enough money and fewer financial worries you can live happier. Money can't buy everything, but it can buy most things. Money can buy you great life experiences and money can buy you a mental state of calm. I believe that the best use of discretionary money is to buy things or do things that enable life experiences which will give you lasting

189

memories. Money isn't just for wealth building, it's for having fun with and enjoying your life. Use money wisely so you can afford to buy what does make you happy.

What money Can and Can't buy Worksheet

What are the things YOU believe money **can't** buy?_____

Why?_____

What are the things YOU believe money **can** buy?_____

Why?_____

Do you believe that money can make you happier? How and why?_____

What is important to you in life?_____

Can money facilitate it?_____

How?_____

What have been the best purchases of your life?_____

Why?_____

What have been the most memorable experiences of your life?_____

Did money facilitate those experiences? How?_____

How will you better use money to bring happiness and experiences into your life?_____

Do you ever participate in a barter system?_____

Would bartering be beneficial for you?_____

Has bartering ever built friendships for you or expanded your network of people?_____

How can you better use bartering? Doing what and for what?_____

How will you use money to make you happy?_____

Chapter #11

<u>Investing Basics</u>

"You can't win if you're not in the game."

I said early in this book that money is worthless until it is spent, invested or leveraged. If money is just sitting there not being put to some use, then it's worthless. This chapter is focused on putting your money to work for you through investing it. The most common way to invest is through financial instruments like stocks, bonds, commodities and mutual funds.

A lot of people don't invest, especially in financial instruments, because they think it's complicated or confusing. Living broke isn't very confusing or complicated and it doesn't require much knowledge. But a little knowledge and dedication with investing will bring huge returns and rewards for you. Investments aren't scary once you understand them and the risks involved. I won't be giving you stock tips or systems of trading, but I will be giving you some simple investment ideas that anyone can do and use to build their wealth.

Investing is NOT a onetime event, it's something you'll do all of your life if you want to build and then preserve your wealth. If you're hoping to make a single huge hit with a onetime investment, then go buy a lottery ticket or dump all your money at a casino. Even stock day traders and hedge fund managers (who trade daily), are in this for the long haul.

You might be lucky enough to invent something, inherit a boatload of money or make a huge financial hit, but then you'll need to invest your money so it continues to grow, or it's at least preserved and protected. It's a terrible feeling to make a ton of money only to spend it all and wind up living broke again.

The meaning of investing. The dictionary gives the following definitions for the word "invest": (1) To put money to use, by purchase or expenditure, in something offering profitable returns, especially interest or income. (2) A devoting, using, or giving of time, talent, emotional energy or money, as for a purpose or to achieve something.

I would like to expand on these definitions for how I'll be using the word in the context of this book. An *investment* is something you buy today with the intent of selling it for a profit at some point in the future. You want to *realize* a gain. Realizing a gain is done by eventually selling what you have purchased—for a profit—and using the money for something else, or, leveraging against your *unrealized* profit (your worth) to buy something or to make further investments. An investment (or worth) is worthless unless it is realized or leveraged. I will cover leveraging later in the chapter. But first…

The mystery of disappearing money:

Ever notice that if you don't specifically do something with your money that it magically disappears? Any extra cash that you have in your pocket just migrates to somewhere, but where? It migrates towards an extra cup of coffee or biscuit at Starbucks, a Honeybun when you're paying for gas or some other random impulsive purchase while you're standing in line at the grocery store. It's easy to have $10, $20 or $100 disappear every week on random impulsive purchases. This really adds up over months and years. Einstein pointed out that small numbers, accumulated and compounded over time, create big numbers. You can use this same powerful mathematical equation of small numbers compounding over time to make your disappearing money add up into a sizeable investment account.

I know I mentioned my past drinking problem a few times in the book, but I think it's important to repeat it in this section. I want to illustrate how "disappearing money," when collected and compounded over time, adds up to BIG numbers.

When I stopped drinking 9 years ago I decided to do something with the money I was **no longer spending** on booze. I did a little math and I figured that I was spending an average of at least $10 a day on my drinking habit. (And that was a conservative estimate.) I realized that if I didn't specifically do something with "my booze money" it would magically disappear. I knew that I would simply spend it on something else. So I started a "Sobriety Savings Account." Every day I would go to the bank and put the $10 **I didn't spend on drinking** into my sobriety savings account. After weekends or Holidays I would deposit the appropriate amount. (The bank doesn't care how often you come in to make a deposit—that's what they're in business for.)

After I had saved up a little over $1,000 (in less than 4 months), I transferred that money into a mutual fund. Then I signed up to make automatic monthly deposits into that mutual fund ($10 a day=$300 per month). So here I am, 9-½ years later, and my "Sobriety Savings" has accumulated into a little over **$40,000**. That's $40,000 I have accumulated, in small increments, just for not drinking and then doing something with the money I no longer spend on booze. That's the power of small numbers accumulating and compounding over time.

Compounding returns:

Why not take advantage of the same mathematical system credit card companies and loan companies use to make big money off of you? In the case of credit cards, your debt is compounded by the interest they charge and then they charge you interest on the interest. Clearly, big companies know the power of compounding small amounts over time and you should use that same power in your favor. In the examples I will be giving you I'm going to be using basic, straight-line compounding. I cannot give you exact figures of outcomes for your individual investments. There are too many variables such as interest rates, when interest is compounded, dividends, when dividends are paid and posted, whether dividends are reinvested, dates that investments are purchased or withdrawn. But don't let these variables scare you away from investing.

Many people have never had a savings account, investment account, brokerage account or 401(K). But you don't need a lot of money to start building your wealth. And I believe you'll find it to be fun to watch your own money grow once you do start.

Begin with a savings account. You can use a bank, Credit Union, whatever. You can also start a savings account at a brokerage like T. Rowe Price, Schwab, Fidelity. If you use a brokerage house, that savings account will be in the form of a Money Market account. Then set up an automatic withdrawal so that every time you get a paycheck, a specific amount goes into savings ($25, $50, $75, $100—the most you can afford). This is an "expenditure" that should be part of your budget plan.

Once you have enough in savings (say $1,000), you switch that into investments such as Index Funds or Sector Funds. After you've educated yourself on how financial instruments work, you may want to begin buying individual stocks. I'm focusing on stocks here because Bonds are more conservative and are typically used by people who already have a lot of wealth and want to preserve and protect their wealth but receive a guaranteed return.

Take advantage of every opportunity your employer offers you to save or invest money. 401(K), 403(B), Christmas Accounts, etc. Many employers offer different types investment matching plans. If your employer offers some sort of "matching," take advantage of it. This truly is FREE money. This is how "matching" works: For instance, every dollar you have deducted from your check and directed into your 401(K), your employer will match it with .50 cents. Some employers offer equal matching. Even if your employer doesn't offer any matching plan, you may want to participate in their investment program. The money will be deducted right off your paycheck and you'll get used to not having it. This is an easy way to invest and build wealth for people who don't want to spend the time to research brokerages, funds and fund types, or who don't have the self-discipline to do automatic investing on their own.

There are a few drawbacks to employer investment plans. They don't always offer the widest variety of investment options and the management fees of the funds you can choose from are typically high. Changing funds within the plan or withdrawing money may be cumbersome or unavailable. If you leave the company or get fired, you'll have to make sure that your 401(K) money is properly transferred to avoid penalties, taxes or fees. Matching plans also have limits as to how much an employer will contribute. Your employer may only "match" up to 3% of your gross pay. So if you earn $30,000 a year and direct $5,000 into your 401(K), that employer will only contribute $900. ($900 is still a lot of FREE money.) Additionally, you want to know when the employer makes his contribution. Is it every pay period, every quarter or at the end of the year? Knowing how much they will match and when it happens helps you decide how much to have deducted and when. If you work at a large company ask the HR director these questions. Or you can call the financial company who handles your company's employee program. It's YOUR money, don't be afraid to ask questions.

I feel you should have the maximum amount your employer will match deducted and directed into your investment plan. If you can afford more, then start your own account at a brokerage that you like. I further believe that you will serve yourself better in the long run if you sign up for an automatic monthly investment plan with a brokerage and then choose the funds which are best for you. This method gets you more involved in your investments and it's much easier to make adjustments, change funds or withdraw money. But if your employer does offer 401(K) "Matching," by all means participate in it. Don't pass on FREE money.

What about taxes? Employer 401(K) and 403(B) programs are usually pre-tax. This means you don't pay income tax on the amount deposited UNTIL you withdraw it. But if you leave the company or get fired and don't properly transfer the money, it will be "distributed" to you. You will pay an early withdrawal penalty and have to pay taxes. You will likely end up with less than you paid in. And far too many people use their 401(K) money for "emergencies." The same early withdrawal penalty and taxes will apply. Don't rob yourself by doing this. I'll explain later how to "use" your 401(K) money without depleting the account or paying penalties and taxes.

There are also different types of IRAs which you can opt for (Traditional or ROTH). Each of these has different tax implications and withdrawal guidelines. IRA accounts do have some advantages and some disadvantages. I'm not going to suggest which is best for you. Do your own research and decide for yourself. I personally do all of my investing with after-tax money and no IRA accounts. That way if I need to access funds or make an emergency withdrawal I don't have to be concerned with penalties or taxes; I've already given the government their piece of the action. It's my money and I can do whatever I want with it whenever I want. Just because I do it that way doesn't mean it's right or that's how you should do it. Educate yourself about IRAs and decide for yourself.

You can't invest without money and you can't earn if you're not invested. All investments are a 50-50 proposition. They will either go up or they will go down, which way do you want to bet? And yes, it is a bet. The two emotions that are often stirred up by money (and investing) are fear and greed. Both can lead to making bad investments. Greed can motivate you to chase unrealistic returns and make risky investments. Fear can hold you back from reaping reasonable returns and investing in the first place. Fear is often the result of lacking knowledge. A person might say, "I have no idea how to invest my money or where to put it." Fear holds people back from investing.

Even if you're terrified of investing and have no knowledge of investment instruments, at the very least START A SAVINGS ACCOUNT! Make regular deposits into your savings account. Saving MUST become part of your budget, even if it's only $10 a month. C'mon you can spare $10 a month towards your own financial wellbeing. Think about how much random crap you buy. You CAN come up with $10 a month. It may not be a lot but it will add up and you'll be building a security net for yourself.

Let's review what happens with $10 a month into a Money Market savings at 1.5% interest. Again, not a lot of money with a high interest return, but after 10 years you'll have $1,306.91. Increase that amount to $50 a month and after 10 years you'll have $6,534.55. If you can afford to put $100 a month into an Index Fund through a brokerage, after 10 years you'll have $17,864.66. That's a profit of $5,764.66 for not spending some of your own money on random crap. For someone who has never had a savings account and has lived broke all of their life, any of these figures is a lot of money. It may be just what you need to feel comfortable knowing you can pay for an emergency, and that money is in YOUR account in YOUR name.

I just gave examples of a 10 year timeframe, but most people reading this will have a 20 to 30 year timeframe for investing. Over 20 years you can build up a sizeable amount. Look what I did in 9-½ years with my sobriety savings account. If you start an Index Fund account with $1,000 and deposit $100 a month, and in 20 years you'll be worth $58,301.25. Want to be worth a half million dollars? Start an Index Fund with $1,000 and deposit $300 per month and in 33 years you'll be worth $503,982.34.

Again I want to point out that the examples I'm showing you are through the use of straight-line compounding. The average return of 7.5% is conservative. The S&P 500 has averaged (over the past 20+ years) a 10% return. I'm also not showing what happens when you receive dividends and automatically reinvest those dividends (DRIP=Dividend Reinvestment Plan). With dividends and enabling a DRIP, instead of taking dividends in cash), your compounded value would be considerably higher.

There's nothing in this for me if you start building up your savings and eventually amass enough to start investing. I get no residuals or royalties from your wealth. I hated living broke and I know that you will feel better about your own life when you have a financial safety net. And the only way to build wealth is to invest your money on a regular basis and allow compounding returns to work magic in your favor.

On to Investing: People like to have their "Virtual Portfolio" online, they track all these different stocks. I caution people about getting overconfident with their "Virtual Portfolio." This isn't a computer game—**this is real money**—your money. People are so proud of the results they get in their virtual portfolio. "I'm up over 60 grand in the virtual portfolio I setup online." All I can say is, "Well then you take your $60,000 virtual profit and see if you can go buy a car with it." Everything changes when you put real money on the table. You'll be watching every ½ penny movement once you buy a stock (stocks do trade in fractions of pennies). Virtual portfolios **aren't real money**—only real money is money.

Investing isn't a part-time job. If you don't have the time to spend and the money to lose, then follow as simple of an investment strategy as possible. I'm not trying to talk you out of tracking stocks, buying individual stocks, bonds, commodities or currencies. But you really should gain some knowledge before placing your own money at risk. Even if you don't trade options you should understand what they are. You should know the difference between a PUT and a CALL option and what terms like: strike price, expiration date, open interest, covered, naked, premium, shorting and short covering mean. This will help you better understand (and hopefully profit from), the fluctuations of a given stock. Fluctuations can and do happen for no apparent reason even when you do understand these terms.

Investing in individual stocks and commodities can be gut wrenching. I have earned a pretty good living for many years doing this, but it is NOT for the weak stomached, and I can assure you that you WILL lose money or at least value on some of your individual positions. This is why I suggest you stick with index funds and mutual funds. You can't be a part-time stock broker. That would be like me trying to be a part-time dentist. I wouldn't be very good at it and somebody is going to get hurt. If you happen to like a certain company then buy some stock and just hold it. Remember that this is NOT a game—it's real money, your money.

Do you want to be an **active** or **passive** investor? I would be considered an active investor because that's how I earn my living. I'm trading something almost every day. However, there may be weeks when I don't make a single sell or buy. But I'm still watching the market. Then suddenly all hell breaks loose and I may make 20 or 30 trades in one day and earn my monthly income in one day. But even when people ask me how they can do what I do, I tell them, "Don't do it! This isn't a game. You're better off buying into index funds, mutual funds or individual stocks that you like and then leaving it alone."

Here's a sample of a typical conversation I have with people about investing:

Bob: How do I get rich?
Mark: Earn a lot of money.
Bob: No, seriously. How do I get rich in the stock market?
Mark: How much do you want to earn?
Bob: I don't know, a lot.
Mark: Well, you really do need to have some idea of how much you want to earn, over what period of time and how much you have to invest.
Bob: Look, I just want to get rich. How do I do it?

That's how many conversations about investing go, and then nothing ever comes of it because most people don't have, or want to have, the patience to let things grow and spend the time to learn the nuances of investing. They don't want to slowly and steadily earn and build wealth, they want to make a big "hit" and suddenly become rich.

But if you really insist on becoming an active investor as a way to earn a living, I want you to consider a few points. If you already have a job that pays $20,000 a year or more, then keep your job and be a passive investor. Unless you have at least $200,000 to tie up or to lose, be a passive investor. Here's why: Even the best money managers have a hard time earning 10% annual returns. This means that if you can earn 10% you'll have not only done better than most money managers, you'll have to have $200,000 invested just to earn $20,000 a year. And how do you plan on earning that $20,000? Through dividends, realized capital gains achieved through short-term trading or a combination of both? Oh, and you'll also have to pay taxes on those dividends and capital gains, so you'll also want to learn about tax law and legal methods for minimizing tax liability. This isn't a game!

To earn money in any investment you need to answer some direct questions, and then based on your answers, evaluate what might be the wisest investment instrument. Here are some of the questions you must answer:

- Exactly how much money or wealth do you want to accumulate?
- Do you want to earn income for spending or do you want to grow portfolio value?
- How much money are you willing and able to invest?
- How much time, realistically, do you have to let this money be tied up in investments?

When you have solid answers to these questions you'll have a better idea of what you might want to invest in and how much you'll need to have invested. Let me give a generalized example for a passive investor.

In this example the person says, "I want to accumulate $500,000 by the time I retire. That will be in 25 years. I earn $40,000 a year. How do I do this?" Using those figures and timeframe we can come up with a plan.

Going with a basic equation of simple compounding returns of 7.5% (average), this person would need to make an initial investment of $10,000 into an index fund like the S&P 500, and then deposit $500 per month into that fund for the next 25 years. This would get them to a total of $485,237.11 at retirement. This final amount would be considerably higher if they were invested in stocks or mutual funds that paid quarterly dividends and those dividends were automatically reinvested.

To really drive the point home, it would cost them $160,000 of their own money (spread out in deposits over 25 years) to walk away with $485,237. That's a **profit of $325,237**. That's making your money work for YOU.

What is the best investment for you?

Once again this is all subjective. Some people don't trust or don't like the stock market, so real-estate might be more in their comfort zone. But real-estate will require money, time and labor. Being a landlord isn't for everyone. Flipping houses isn't as profitable and easy as it sounds. Some people buy precious metals or jewels, others like a good old-fashioned savings account at a bank.

There is risk to every investment and there is a cost (the transaction expense or management fee), involved in every investment purchase. Even if you were to buy physical gold, you will have to store it securely somewhere (which may be a cost), and while you're waiting for it to appreciate in value—that's if it does go up in value—you won't be earning dividends or interest while your gold is collecting dust. And you won't make any money until you sell your gold.

I'll say it again. There is risk to investing. You CAN lose money. Most people who lose money do so out of fear. It's not fun to see the value of your fund or stock decrease in value, but you actually haven't lost anything until you make the decision to sell at a loss. Conversely, you haven't made (or realized) any profit until you actually sell the investment at a gain. There are many opinions and strategies as to when to sell or buy. Plenty of books and websites tout systems, technical analysis, charts and strategies; most are personal beliefs and gut feelings. I am an active trader and I feel most people are best served to be "buy and hold" investors.

Far too many financial advisers will tell you, "Your investment doesn't keep pace with inflation." Having your investments keep pace with inflation is a nice reference point, but in many ways it's not important. Don't let that statement about "keeping pace with inflation" distract you from what makes you comfortable, or drive you to buy into overly risky investments. A savings account doesn't keep pace with inflation, but it sure is nice to have money available if you need it in an emergency. Even if your investment account were to stay flat for 10 years, as long as you keep putting money into it every month, at the end of 10 years you will have amassed a sizeable nest egg. If you don't save or invest you'll have nothing at the end of 10 years. If you don't have a savings account or investments, then you are absolutely NOT keeping pace with inflation. Would you rather have some money and investments stashed away for retirement or none at all?

The least complicated way to invest is by using index funds or mutual funds. Index funds track and follow (in value) the various indexes. Put simply, if you are invested in a Dow Jones index fund and the Dow average goes up, your fund value goes up the same percentage amount. With index funds you don't have to buy an equal weighting (amount) of all the stocks listed in that index, the Dow Jones 30 for example. Index funds also have lower annual management fees. This is capitalism, so every fund or financial instrument has fees for getting in, maintaining your account and getting out. These fees and annual maintenance charges can lower your returns considerably over time. I'm cheap and I want the lowest costs available. Index funds do just that.

This chapter is limited in scope, so I will list some examples of index funds. But I want YOU to do some research and begin expanding your knowledge of the various funds. Some index funds are: Dow Jones Average, Dow Jones Transportation, S&P 500, Russell 2000, Wilshire 5000, NASDAQ 100, NASDAQ 10000.

Then there are also "Sector" and "Specialty" mutual funds. These funds will focus on specific industry types such as: Telecommunications, Recreation, Medical, Pharmaceuticals, Social Media, Retail, Technology, Energy, etc. Specialty funds may buy stock in many different industries but have a specific focus such as dividends, capital appreciation or guaranteed income through bonds. There are thousands of mutual funds on the market. Each of these funds has a person and most likely a staff managing them and those people want to earn money, so that's where management fees come into play.

If you like a certain industry type such as social media, medical companies, energy companies or technology, or you have a gut feeling for a certain business sector, you will find a mutual fund that covers it. There are also mutual funds that focus on humanistic factors, such as only buying stock in green companies, Christian founded companies and funds that won't buy any "sin stocks" like tobacco, alcohol, gambling or firearms. You can still invest while following your own moral compass. Whatever type of fund you plan on buying always look at the management fees. Some fees can be as high as 2.5% annually. That may not sound like a lot, but over time those higher fees really eat up your gains. Conversely, the lowest fee doesn't necessarily mean it's the best fund to invest in.

As I said, there is limited scope to what I can cover in this chapter. There are plenty of good books out there that explain mutual funds, how they work and what to look for in a good fund. There are also many reputable brokerage firms that offer mutual funds along with very comprehensive research and educational tools on their websites. Naturally these firms want you to invest your money through them so they will always reflect their unique funds in the best light. But most financial firms do offer index funds and the management fees on index funds will be lower than their managed funds. I make no personal recommendations, but T. Rowe Price, Vanguard, Fidelity and Schwab are highly reputable companies. I don't want to disclose who I use as a brokerage because I don't want it to be misconstrued as an endorsement. This is YOUR money so take the time to take this seriously. Spend the time to do some research before you spend your money.

Do what you do best; work at your job, career, occupation, whatever you want to call it. Earn a regular income and direct 10 to 15% of your income towards savings and investments. Unless you're a broker, fund manager or financial director, just go do your job and let your money work for you through simple investments. It doesn't matter whether you're a plumber, factory laborer, office worker, IT specialist, dental hygienist—any occupation—you CAN build wealth by saving and investing.

What will you invest in? I want you to think which is best for you; savings account, index funds, mutual funds, individual stocks, bonds, commodities, precious metals, real-estate? Your investment goals, risk tolerance and strategies will likely change over time. It's in your own best interest to be flexible with your investments. You may start out buying older homes, refurbishing them and then renting them out. If you get tired of being a landlord or it's not as profitable as you thought, then move your money into other investments. If you don't want to do a lot of active buying and selling of investments, then focus your investment money into index funds. At the very least you must begin with a savings account so that you'll have some money to invest with.

Some people are afraid of the stock market, they claim that it's rigged. I have a couple schools of thought on this. The first is like claiming that casinos are rigged. The reputable ones aren't. They don't have to rig their games. Human nature rigs it for them. People will gladly throw their money at a gamble, hoping for a big return. Someone may go on a hot winning streak for a while but the casino knows that that person will lose it all back. How many people ever walk into a casino, place a $1,000 bet at a Blackjack table and walk away if they win? They have a 50-50 chance to double their money in one hand of Blackjack. If they do win and double their money they keep playing until the profits and their original $1,000 is gone. Professional gamblers who do it for a living earn a small but reasonable return and walk away to play another day. That's what investing is like. Go for small but reasonable returns and come back to play another day.

Stocks can be the same way. People either want to make a big hit on one stock or they have a good run and think they can't do wrong—only to buy into wild positions and lose it all. Regardless of whether you're a "buy and hold" investor or trade daily, be in this for the long run. Earn reasonable returns and be in a position to play again another day.

Even though investments are gambling, the stock market is far different from a casino. When you lose money in the stock market you haven't lost it back to the house (conmen and crooks like Bernie Madoff aside). There is no one sitting in an office watching you on a closed-circuit camera as you lose money. Wall Street is a place where floor traders and financial companies do their business. In the scheme, Wall Street is word, not a person or an individual company.

So who profits if **YOU** lose money in the stock market? No one individual may directly profit from your loss. Let me give you an example. Let's say that I buy a stock for $8 a share and I sell it for $10 a share. That's a $2 per share profit for me. You buy the stock that I just sold for $10 and it continues to go up and you sell it for $13 a share, a $3 per share profit. (By the way, when you bought the stock you didn't buy it directly from me, this wasn't a private transaction.)

I think the stock will continue going up so I buy it again at $13. (I didn't buy it from you, I bought it from the "float," shares that are publicly floating for trading.) But the stock goes down instead. It's now back to $10 a share. I may have lost *value* but I haven't lost any real money unless I sell it. But the stock continues to go down further, I get scared and I **do** sell it at $9 a share. I have just lost $4 a share in my real money, but no one took $4 from me—not you, not my broker, not Wall Street, no one. Someone else simply bought the stock from the "float" which I willingly sold into the "float" at $9. The stock continues going down and whoever bought it from me at $9 sells it for $7 a share, but they didn't lose $2 a share to me—I didn't profit from their loss. Suddenly the stock shoots back up to $13 and whoever bought the stock at $7 just earned $6 a share (but only if they sell it to someone else). In this example, no one individual—even evil Wall Street—directly *took* money away from anyone who sold at a loss. Every transaction was done willingly. Some transactions were profitable, others weren't.

As a side note to this example, had I just held on to the stock (which I recommend most people should do), I would have watched my *value* go down by $1 a share only to see my *value* increase by $5 a share. But instead, a series of transactions took place, moved by fear and greed, which resulted in profits for some and losses for others.

But let's go back to the casino comparison. What if the roulette wheel (or stock market) *is* rigged? You can still win. Just watch and figure out how it's rigged and bet with the rig to make it work in your favor. But be cautious about finding the "rig" in the market or a casino. What you think is a pattern or a rig may be wishful thinking or a short-term anomaly. The mind can find correlations and patterns in anything. Hell, you can find a pattern in vomit if you look hard enough (but why?). So use index funds to bet with the "rig." Why? Because all of those evil Wall Street fund managers want to see the indexes go up.

There will always be crooks and market manipulators, but for the most part, I believe that financial markets are a legitimate way to invest. Fear and greed is what moves markets. Fear causes people to irrationally sell. Greed causes people to irrationally buy. These emotions cause market fluctuations. When people ask me what I do for a living I say, "I buy fear and sell greed." My philosophy is: "When all the rats are jumping ship, buy the ship. The rats will want to get back on again at some time."

Make the investment choices that are within your comfort zone. Be willing to make adjustments as your life needs change, but stay your course. Long-term "buy and hold" investors have built a lot of wealth for themselves. They've done this through employer sponsored 401(K) or 403(B) programs and by having dedication to making regular deposits into their investment accounts.

And the rich get richer:

How does this happen? It isn't because all rich people are lucky nor is it because every rich person is greedy and evil. Rich people leverage their money. They borrow against their wealth to increase their wealth. I'll give some examples and tell you how you can do the same thing.

Let's say that I own 1,000 shares of a stock that is consistently trading at $80 a share. I purchased the stock 3 years ago at $70 a share. I have an *unrealized* gain of $10,000 and a value of $80,000 but I have no actual profit or cash unless I sell it. I don't want to sell the stock because I like the company, I want to stay invested and it also happens to pay a nice annual dividend of $2.56 per share (3.2% yield). Every 3 months I receive a check for $640 which I can spend. (If I opted for a DRIP I would acquire more shares every 3 months, resulting in even more dividends every 3 months—the power of compounding.) But I like getting a check that I can spend towards my living expenses.

Because I own the stock through a brokerage, I have a value of $80,000 with that brokerage and I can leverage (margin) against that value. But I will have to pay interest on whatever amount I borrow, and I also don't want to (or can't), borrow more than 50% of the value. That means in this case I can borrow up to $40,000 from the brokerage who is holding my stock, and use that money to either buy more stock, a different stock, some other type of investment or use the cash to buy something else for me personally. The interest I pay to the brokerage is an investment expense and therefore a deduction from my investment earnings.

But leveraging can also be a risky proposition. If I borrow against my $80 stock but the stock craters and loses 40% of its value, suddenly my stock is only worth $48,000 (margin power of $24,000), but I've already borrowed $40,000 against it. That means I have to come up with $16,000 to give back to the brokerage, or sell some stock to cover the difference. This is termed as the dreaded "margin call." Then everything can begin cascading into a downhill spiral. Being leveraged too far is how some people get ruined in the market. It's also a catalyst in certain market crashes.

A housing bubble is an example of this. If someone owns one house they can borrow against that house to buy another one. They can keep borrowing and amassing real-estate as long as the housing market is strong. But when housing prices begin to drop, people who own leveraged property have to start selling their houses. Suddenly there are more sellers than buyers and prices go down even further, but the leveraged property owner still has to pay off or make monthly payments on these houses. Then bankruptcy and foreclosures skyrocket and the bubble bursts.

This also happens with stock market crashes. If a lot of people are leveraged too far and prices of stocks start dropping, they'll have to sell stock to cover what they owe. But there will be more sellers than buyers and the price of stocks continue to drop. Then more people want to sell their stock—the rats start jumping ship—and then the market crashes hard.

210

Being margined or leveraged can be just as anxiety-laden as being broke and you do run the risk of losing everything if your leverage or margin is "called in." Leverage and margin are like credit cards—when used wisely they are a great way to take advantage of credit, but just like credit cards, you can't get carried away with your purchases.

Here's how the average person can leverage. If you have a 401(K), 403(B) or holdings in a brokerage account, you may be able to borrow against it. But don't just borrow for the sake of having money to spend. Let's say you need a new car or want to pay for night classes to further your education. Instead of getting a traditional auto loan or student loan, you *could* borrow against your holdings. You will have to pay the loan back and pay interest, but you are borrowing from yourself without selling or redeeming any of your investments. Not every 401(K), 403(B) or brokerage allows for this option. You'll have to do some checking into it. And you also need to consider the risk and anxiety. It may be less stressful for you to opt for a traditional loan.

Taking out a second mortgage or home equity line of credit is another way people leverage. These types of loans are meant to be used for home improvements to increase the resale value of the home. But most of the money borrowed with these loans is spent on everything *but* home improvements. People use home equity loans to buy cars, boats, luxury items and consumables. The monthly payments may be low, often with differed principal in the case of interest only loans, and the interest on the loan is used as a tax deduction. But when the "secured" property is sold, that second mortgage or home equity loan must be paid off, leaving less for the seller if not even being a negative balance, termed "being under water."

Here's an example: You bought your home for $120,000 and you owe $100,000 on your mortgage. Home values in your area have gone up and your home is valued at $150,000. You don't want to sell your home but you would like a new car, a vacation and some other pleasantries. Your home is worth $150,000 and you owe $100,000—you technically have $50,000 worth of equity. You can borrow (leverage) against that equity, so you take on a home equity line of credit.

You don't want to get carried away with your spending so you only borrow $30,000. You buy a car, take a vacation, get a new TV, some furniture and appliances, maybe even pay off some credit card bills. As it stands now, you owe a total of $130,000 on your home. This may not be a problem providing that you don't get laid off, have to pay for a major home repair, some other large expense or don't have to move. But if something unexpected happens you may have to sell your home, and sell it for less than what you think it's worth or would like to get.

Unexpectedly you do end up in a position where you have to sell your home and it turns out that you're only able to get $135,000. After closing costs and other required improvements or conditions of sale, you net (receive) $131,000. Because you owed $130,000 ($100,000 to the mortgage company and $30,000 to the bank for your home equity loan) you walk away with only $1,000 after all secured loans are paid. You don't even get your down payment money back. But what if you're only able to get $125,000 for the sale of your home? You owe $130,000 so you will have to pay $5,000 at closing to satisfy the loans against your home. If you can't come up with the extra $5,000 you can't sell your home, you're "under water." You may have to default and walk away with nothing or go further into debt just to sell your home.

Leveraging is a delicate house of cards, but used prudently it can allow you to use your own wealth to build more wealth or access credit without divesting or depleting your wealth. I'm NOT suggesting that you do or don't use margin, leverage home equity or borrow against your investment holdings. I'm simply explaining how it's done and how the wealthy use their wealth to further increase their wealth.

This chapter is intended to enlighten you about investing and get you interested in it. The average worker **can** build wealth through conservative and passive investing, as long as they do it on a regular basis and let compounding work in their favor. Please don't let your money mysteriously disappear from your pockets. Put "unused" money to work instead of randomly spending it on impulsive purchases. Remember that small numbers add up to BIG numbers over time. If you don't know what type or level of wealth you want you won't know how much or what to invest in. Every investment entails some level of risk. If you are highly risk averse then at the very least invest in a traditional savings account at a bank or credit union. Some money in savings is better than no money at all, even if doesn't keep up with inflation. Most of us must work for our money. Turn that around and make your money work for YOU. Money is worthless until you spend it, invest it or leverage it. Why not spend some of your own money on investing into your own wealth?

<u>Your investment Worksheet:</u>

Do you fear investing? Why?_____

Do you have the patience to invest and let the power of compounding work for you?_____

Would you prefer to be an active or passive investor?_____

Do you have an investment plan? What is it?_____

Have you answered the questions about how wealthy you want to be?_____

Do you have realistic expectations of how wealthy you can be based on how much you have to invest?_____

Do you want to earn money to spend now or are you looking to build wealth to spend at a future time?_____

Are you going to take investing seriously? What research are you going to do? How will you educate yourself?_____

Do you personally know people who have built wealth through investments? How did they do it? What type of investments? Can you ask them about it? Can you learn from them?_____

Does your employer offer a 401(K) or 403(B) investment plan? Are you participating in it?_____

What % of your pay can and will you apply towards an employer investment plan?_____

Does your employer offer an investment matching plan? What is the plan? What is the maximum amount your employer will contribute? Will you participate up to that maximum?_____

Do you have a good understanding of leveraging and how it works? Is that something you would be comfortable doing? If you use leverage or margin, what would you use it for?_____

Do you believe you can become wealthy with a simple and conservative investment plan?_____

Chapter #12

Final Details and Insurances.

"I'm too young to need a will. I'll worry about that if I get rich or when I'm old."

Building your own financial security and wealth requires that you also think about some other uncomfortable questions. I don't want to make this chapter too morbid, but it's very important that you think about what will happen with your assets and belongings *after* you're gone. The fact is that none of us will get out of here alive and you've worked too hard during your life to acquire money, assets and other personal property. I'm sure you don't want to have all of your accumulated wealth wasted by careless heirs, have your money or stuff going to the wrong people, or worse yet, being taken by the government because you made no provisions or stipulations to protect it.

I want to state that the scope of this chapter won't, and can't answer all of your questions about what's the best plan for you to have in place, but I hope it will get you thinking and doing some deeper research of your own. Reviewing your assets, planning for your final wishes and creating a directive is an eye-opening exercise. You'll get a chance to look at your own life and what you've accomplished so far. This may help motivate you to make bigger and better plans for what you'll do in the future. It will also cause you to think about the important people in your life and what they mean to you.

You're never too young or too poor to have life insurance, a will and directives for distribution of your assets. None of us know when we'll be leaving the planet and it's not very costly or time consuming to make preparations. As your life moves along you will likely acquire financial assets and various material belongings that are special to you which you would like to pass along to specific people or organizations. You will also acquire debt and other financial obligations. If something untimely happens to you before your "golden years" you want to make sure that your spouse, children, family or friends aren't burdened with your bills or debts. Your death will be hard enough for your loved ones to cope with, leaving them with uncertainty and financial burdens to bear will make it even worse.

I have been involved in the disbursement and closing out of estates for both elderly and young people. Having directions and money available to clear up the last of their affairs absolutely does make the grieving less painful, especially if it's a sudden or untimely death. I'm not talking about inheritance money here, I'm talking about having life insurance money or other funds available for settling their bills, paying for apartment or home cleaning, distribution or disposal of their personal belongings and of course their funeral expenses. It costs time and money to close out someone's life. When someone has sufficient life insurance and clear directives of "who gets what and what's to be done with my body," it makes it less stressful to distribute and dispose of their belongings along with fulfilling their wishes for their final interment. I feel it's an act of love and caring on the part of the deceased to make these preparations.

You might not think you have enough money or stuff to concern yourself with a will right now. But I would like you to think about who would take care of closing out your accounts, distributing and disposing of your possessions and paying off your bills if you were to suddenly wake up dead one morning. (Only in my drinking days do I remember waking up dead.) Even if you don't go through an attorney to have a legal will drawn up, you should at the very least have a couple of pages, written and signed by you and a witness, describing how you want your possessions distributed. Put those pages in a sealed envelope and place it somewhere someone could easily find it, or ask a trusted family member or friend if they are willing to be your executor and leave the sealed envelope with them. Your "executor" is the person who will be authorized, by you, to be in complete control of all your accounts, final details and the carrying out of your wishes after you're gone.

What should be written in your directives document? It should be addressed to your executor. I feel that you should write your document as if you were talking to your executor. It doesn't require all sorts of fancy words and legal mumbo-jumbo. The simpler the better so there isn't any confusion. You should clearly state what you want done with your remains (your body). Knowing what you want done after death will give you a better idea of how much life insurance coverage you'll need to cover these costs.

You might have some items that aren't of great financial value but are of high personal value to you or others, then list them. Your nephew Andy might really admire your sports paraphernalia collection, then state that you want him to have it. i.e. "I would like my nephew Andy Smith to receive all of my sports cards, posters, shirts and commemorative balls. This includes any item that has a team logo on it."

If you don't clearly write out what you want done with your possessions who knows how or where they'll be disposed of. For instance, if I'm the executor of your affairs and your cousin Bob comes along and tells me, "You know, Jeff wanted me to have his coin collection and his motorcycle," all I can say is, "Well, I understand your request, however, neither of those were listed specifically in his directives. If I don't have to liquidate either of them to pay expenses we'll have to discuss it with the immediate next of kin once all other bills have been satisfied." Cousin Bob may get very angry with me because he insists Jeff told him that. And Jeff *may* have told him that, but I as the executor have no written documentation supporting Bob's claim.

Or there may be disputes between the remaining vultures. Cousin Ken insists that Jeff wanted *him* to get the motorcycle, suddenly Bob and Ken get into an argument over it, pinning me in the middle. As executor I would rather be able say, "I'm sorry Ken but Jeff's directive clearly states that Bob is to receive the motorcycle. If you have a dispute you'll have to bring that up with Bob." My obligation as executor is to close out the estate by first paying required bills and distributing what has been documented in a will or directive. Whatever else is left over will then be at my discretion to distribute. And if I'm not an honest or honorable person I'll have what's left over distributed to me. So choose someone you trust as your executor.

If you plan on keeping your directives document securely locked in a safe or safety deposit box, it isn't a bad idea to list all of your debts, loans, credit cards and asset accounts along with the respective account numbers. This will make it easier for your executor to close out and satisfy all accounts with your name associated to them. Your executor will need to know where this information is and how to access it.

Make things easy on your executor, and for those who survive you, so that your belongings and assets are distributed as you want. Write out a distribution and final services directive. Sign it, date it and have your signature witnessed by someone other than your executor. This doesn't have to be notarized or a fancy legal document. In most cases nothing within your will or directive will be contested. If you are extremely wealthy and have a lot of assets then it is worth the money to have a will and directives drawn up with the services of and held by an attorney.

Adjust your will (or directives) and insurance coverage as your life changes. People come and go in your life, relationships build and some end. If you have someone designated as a beneficiary and they are no longer alive, that money or that item will revert back into your estate and it will be up for grabs to the next of kin or distributed by the executor.

I'm going to talk about changes that took place in my own life and I hope it will spark some ideas that you will be able to apply when writing your own directives and looking at your own life insurance.

When I was 18 and single I joined the military. I took out a small life insurance policy through the military. I made my parents the beneficiaries so they wouldn't be burdened by my debts and my disposal if I died. A few years later I got married, so I changed the beneficiary to my wife. As time went on we bought a home, had a mortgage, auto loans and more debt. I kept my military life insurance but also took out an additional $250,000 life insurance policy with my wife as beneficiary. I didn't want my wife to be in a bad financial spot if I accidentally died. Then, after I was divorced and my mortgages were paid off, I lowered my life insurance to $35,000. I have no debt, no children and no one to provide for, so why should I carry, and keep paying for, a high life insurance policy? However, I do want to make sure that my executor will have enough money available to pay off and clean up any lingering bills (property taxes, utilities, etc.), pay for my cremation and then use whatever might be left over to throw a party. My executor is the beneficiary to my current life insurance policy. If I ever get married again I'll adjust things accordingly. It doesn't cost any money to change the names of beneficiaries on your life insurance policy.

My assets, bills and accounts, along with my personal belongings are all detailed out. I want certain people to have certain items. My executor will see to this and no one can argue or make invalid claims to anything. I do this to simplify the work of my executor and to give me peace of mind knowing that the people I love will receive what I want them to receive.

As I said, I have a very clear-cut and easy to understand will and directives. I update my will and directives every year on my birthday because things change in life. I recently sold my boat, a car, some rental property and other belongings. I also acquired a few belongings in the past year. I don't want my will or directives to be out of date, referring to things which I no longer own or to people who are no longer alive or are part of my life.

You've worked hard for your money and possessions. You've collected or created things that have meaning to you. Make sure that the people you want to have them receive them. Create a will and directives NOW while you still can, because the moment you're dead you will no longer have any say in the matter.

My health insurance plan has also been adjusted over the years. When I was young and single I didn't have very comprehensive coverage. If you're single and in fairly good health, why spend more money on a comprehensive health insurance plan that you may never use? When I got married we adjusted our health insurance plan upwards. At that time I was living an extremely unhealthy lifestyle (heavy drinking and drug use), I saw my doctor frequently and opted for the lowest deductable available. After I quit drinking my health dramatically improved so I didn't need such a comprehensive health insurance plan.

When I became divorced, I ended up with no health insurance. I went the next 6 years without any health insurance at all. I finally HAD to get health insurance, forced upon me by law. So now I waste $2,200 a year for something I don't ever use, but I have peace of mind knowing that I'm protected from financial ruin if something major or catastrophic happens to me. (I admit that it was risky going without health insurance, but I was willing to take the risk. During that time I used the money I didn't spend on health insurance to pay off debts.) Not having health insurance can make you 'broke' if something happens to you. Having health insurance is critical to the protection of your money and assets.

My thoughts on Life Insurance: People have different reasons for carrying life insurance and there are many different life insurance products. Let's first discuss some of the reasons for having life insurance. As I said, it costs money to finalize and close out someone's life such as loans, debts, mortgage and other bills. Depending on what type, if any, memorial service you want, final placement of the corpse or remains costs money. (I hate to sound so morbid but it's the truth—you have to pay someone to do something with the body.)

220

Most people carry life insurance so that they have peace of mind knowing that these various expenses will be paid without their death costing family or friends any of their money. Another reason is to provide for the financial security of the decedents spouse, children or those who were in their care. If you are the owner of a business or a partner in a business you will probably carry some life insurance to cover what the business owes or to compensate your partner(s) for your portion of debt. Life insurance is also used as a way to distribute wealth that the decedent never earned or saved up during their life. I think that last reason is the worst reason to have life insurance—why not earn, enjoy and share your money with the ones you love while you're still alive? Thinking about *why* you want life insurance will give you a better idea of how much coverage you need and what type of life insurance product would be best for you.

You must also be able to qualify for life insurance. This means that you are essentially healthy and do not have pre-existing conditions that could shorten your life such as cancer, diabetes, and a host of others. The insurance industry is a heavily documented and researched collection of data that assesses risk and assign respective costs. It's wise to buy life insurance early in your life when qualification is not a problem and premiums are lower. As you get older the qualification is more difficult due to you age or your health.

There are many different life insurance products. (Some of you may already know this stuff, but play along anyway.) The simplest is called: **Term Life Insurance**. This means you will have coverage for a fixed amount of time, usually for a term of 10 years. The death benefit payout amount remains the same and the annual (or monthly) premium remains the same for the entire "term" of the contract. For example, a 10 year Term policy for $100,000 at age 25 may cost you $22 a month ($264 a year, $2,640 total over 10 years). Not a bad price to pay for $100,000 in peace of mind. If you haven't died after 10 years of initiating the policy, your policy expires and you or your beneficiaries get nothing.

At that point you can renew or get another 10 year Term policy. But because you're 10 years older, and mathematically closer and more likely to becoming dead, the premium will increase. That same $100,000 coverage at age 35 may now cost you $54 a month ($648 a year, $6,480 total). In the example of 10 year term, this premium will continue going up dramatically every 10 years until you become uninsurable. What I mean by uninsurable is that the policy expires or runs out at a predetermined date, such as age 80. Or you're just so old that no one will insure you.

Insurers can also reduce the amount of the death benefit as you get older, depending on how the insurance contract is written. The insurance company is gambling and hoping that you won't die, but they know that eventually you will. That's why the premium goes up and at some point you become uninsurable with "term" insurance. The insurance company would love for you to live a long life because they want to collect thousands of dollars from you for offering you peace of mind and paying your beneficiaries nothing because you stayed alive. Term life insurance is typically the least expensive type of life insurance.

There is also **Whole Life**. There are too many variations on Whole Life plans to discuss them all, but I'll give you examples. Some whole life plans convert into annuities which then, when you turn a certain age they pay you a monthly amount. Some will pay your beneficiaries a monthly amount. Some policies come to maturity on a determined date and you receive a portion or all of your money back, but life insurance coverage is halted. Whole life is also considered as an investment product because if you live long enough you'll get some money back.

Decreasing coverage policy. This means that as time passes (usually by the year), your coverage and premium will be reduced. For instance, if you owe a lot on your mortgage or for a business (let's say $200,000), as you reduce the amount you owe your coverage and premium reduces. Your policy is intended to pay off your debts and issue the balance to beneficiaries. If you reduce your debt to $100,000 your coverage can go down by that amount and your premiums will be less. This type of policy is typically for business owners, partnerships or people with huge mortgages.

Universal Life is really an investment instrument which has a life insurance portion and an investment value. The premium pays for the insurance and a portion is invested generating a cash value assigned to the policy. People who already have a lot of money often buy this type of life insurance product.

It 's worth your time to investigate and learn about all types of life insurance so you can decide which might best fill your needs and which gives you the highest peace of mind.

Here are my suggestions: If you're single and don't have a mortgage or major debts and loans, buy a $25,000 10 year Term life insurance policy. If you do have a home and loans, your life insurance coverage should be equal to (plus $25,000) of what you owe. If your mortgage is currently $75,000 and you have $8,000 auto loan and $3,000 in credit card debt, you'll want $125,000 in coverage. You do this so that in the event of your death the person closing out your affairs isn't scattering to sell things or default on your obligations. Make your untimely passing financially easy on that person.

If you're married or have children, make sure that you have enough coverage so they will be able to pay off the mortgage and have enough left over to pay for future living expenses. A $500,000 or $1,000,000 life insurance policy isn't outrageous in this situation. Large policies can be expensive but you have an obligation to "insure" that your spouse or children don't become destitute if you accidentally or prematurely die.

While I'm talking about life insurance, I want to remind you that you also should have (and are often required to have) **liability insurance** if you own a home or rent a house or apartment. These policies cover you for accidents for injuries on your property and loss of personal belonging through fire, theft or other insurable reasons. These policies come with insured values based on appraisal, deductibles, and other factors such as the neighborhood, whether you have a dog and the breed of dog.

An **Umbrella Policy** covers above and beyond the limits of your other liability policies. An umbrella policy is a separate policy and a supplement to liability insurance covering home and auto. It does not pay off in the case of death and is not associated with life insurance. So if you get sued for more than your current liability coverage, the umbrella kicks in. Umbrella policies that are supplements to existing liability insurance generally start at $1,000,000 in coverage. An umbrella also covers a category called errors and omissions. My opinion is that an Umbrella policy and Universal life are products for people who have $500,000 or more in owned assets.

You may also wish to consider **disability insurance**. I'm not a big fan of this coverage myself. Disability insurance either pays a fixed amount, a percentage of your average wage or a percentage of your bills in the event a major health condition occurs or if an accident renders you unable to work. Again, there are so many variations in "qualified" disabilities and coverage amounts that I can't go over all of them. Disability insurance is often piggybacked onto your life insurance policy and may not cost that much to add it on. But don't just blindly agree to adding it on or paying for it separately. Ask questions and learn what "disability" means within the guidelines of the specific policy, what's covered and what will be paid to you if you sustain an injury or disability. You might think you're covered for an injury to your back, but you're only covered for dismemberment. Ask a lot of questions before you buy.

Many employers automatically give you minimal life and disability insurance coverage as a fringe benefit. However, this coverage ends if you leave the company or get laid off for an extended period of time. You would be wise to see who is named as the beneficiary on such a policy. You might think your loved ones will be taken care of, only for them to find out that they are named as co-beneficiaries. Any employer paid benefit will end when you leave the company or it may be suspended if you don't work enough hours or you're not actively working there for a pre-specified period of time.

There are so many different types of life and disability insurances with varying types of coverage. Before you spend your hard earned money, take the time to learn about some of them. Ask a lot of questions. Ask example styled questions like, "If I die in an accident and the accident is my own fault because I was drunk, does my policy still pay my beneficiaries? (I always asked this question when I was a drinker.) What proof is necessary and how long will it take for the payment? How is the payment disbursed? Is it a single check or a series of checks? Are there or will there be any taxes my beneficiaries will have to pay?" (Typically life insurance payout of a death benefit is tax exempt, however, if it's in the form of an annuity it may be taxable.) Ask a lot of questions before you sign.

My thoughts on health insurance: The ACA or Affordable Care Act (Obamacare) makes this a difficult topic to write about due to employer mandates and individual mandates requiring coverage. You have to have health insurance regardless of your health or employment status. But there are ways to keep your health insurance and health maintenance costs at a minimum. Instead of paying a high monthly premium for comprehensive health insurance with low doctor visit deductibles and complete medication coverage, consider higher deductibles and higher medication co-pay. However, you have to take your current health, your family health history and if you're currently taking high cost prescription medications into consideration. If you're in reasonably good physical condition and live a healthy lifestyle you may want to opt for a higher deductible lower cost health insurance plan.

If you have a spouse or are responsible for children, you have to consider your spouse's health history, the age and health condition of your children. Better health care coverage may cost you more money. Too bad. Your spouse and your children are YOUR responsibility—don't neglect their healthcare coverage.

You can use health insurance to keep yourself and your family healthier at a low cost. Most health insurance plans will pay for regular and preventative checkups. Many will pay a portion of a health club membership or monthly gym dues. Some will even lower your monthly premiums if you are an active member at one of their accredited gyms or health clubs. Health insurance companies want to keep you healthy because it keeps their payout costs down. Take advantage of all health maintenance and health management services offered by your insurer.

Health care insurance is expensive. Don't waste any more money on it than you have to. You can save yourself a lot of money if you do your homework and find the plan that fits your needs and your budget.

I have only scratched the surface of health, disability and life insurance. These are items that you should find out about yourself. Without health insurance you can find yourself broke due to medical bills. Or in the event of your unexpected death, leave your family strapped with your debts if you don't have life insurance. I have purposely avoided giving any strong recommendations of which types of insurances to buy. I don't have to live in your skin, so if you think you should have the fullest medical coverage, disability insurance, whole life or a $2,000,000 term life insurance plan, then buy it. But remember that the higher your coverage (on any insurance) the more you will pay, even if you never use it or need it.

During your lifetime you will spend tens of thousands of dollars on insurance products. Health insurance, life insurance, auto insurance, homeowners or renters insurance are just a few. Insurance protects you from going broke, but you can also end up living broke by overspending on the wrong insurance products. Insurances may be a necessary evil, but the day may come when you're glad you had it. Try to minimize your insurance expenses and get the highest utility out of every penny you spend on it.

It's all a gamble.

Our entire life is a gamble. We bet on careers, relationships and the success of those careers and relationships. We buy insurances betting that we might die, be involved in auto accidents, become sick or disabled. The insurance companies gamble and bet that we won't die, be in auto accidents, become sick or disabled. All insurances are calculated gambles, for both you and the company who insures you.

I find it curious that it is less expensive to insure our health and life while in our youth than when we are older, yet in our youth we often place our health and life in higher risk situations. We can spend less money on insurances in our early years, using our money to live well or amass wealth. As we go through our earning years, most of our time is spent chasing money, acquisitions and personal belongings. Then as we get older, we make plans to distribute all of the money and possessions we've acquired. As we mature into our golden years it will cost more to insure ourselves but we will likely spend less on acquisitions.

Life is such a weird, financially twisted journey. We can only hope that we make the right decisions during our life and hope that all those decisions turn out well. But in the overall, our entire life truly is a gamble.

Part 2

I'm pretty good at quite a few things in life. I'm also pretty good at knowing and accepting what I'm **not good at** and when I should turn to and listen to outside advisers. I am not all that knowledgeable about health care directives, living wills and estate planning when children and dependants are involved. But these are very important topics to discuss. I am turning these topics over to someone who is more knowledgeable on this than I am.

The following segment is a contribution from my friend and financial mentor **Jeff Rendall**. Jeff and I have very similar approaches in that we like to share information with the hope of getting the other person involved in their own education and decision making process. I credit Jeff with prodding me to constantly analyze and reevaluate my approach to financial instruments and life. He has taught me through questions, not by telling me what I should do. He and I have somewhat different styles of investing and viewing life, yet our values and ethics run in unison. I am honored that he would consider me not only a peer but a friend as well.

Taking care of things.

A contribution by: Jeff Rendall

It's nice to get the compliments from Mark as written above. I consider it an important part of my life to provide information to others so they can improve their lives, the lives of the ones they love and those that love them. Sometimes a gift of knowledge is hard to deliver because the subject matter is unpleasant or emotions play a role in honest acceptance of the information. Instead of transferring knowledge through directives, an open ended inquiry to plan for some kind of improvement is a better approach. So as you read the following material, think about how you dealt with the decline in health of a loved one in the past, and ask yourself what you wish might have been done differently to make it easier on all those personally involved. This is a chance for you to turn heartbreak, hardship and confusion about what to do sometime in the future; into an ordered celebration of the end of one life and the continued success of many other lives.

As financial accounts, both taxable and tax exempt accumulate, naming beneficiaries is a critical part of your plan for the future. Minor children under the age of eighteen and other dependents are a part of the plan also. Guardianship in case of your unplanned incapacitation or departure from this world needs thought and direction. Other actions you need to take in the case of the inability to make your own decisions or death; include a health care directive, durable power of attorney, a will (simple or complicated) and other documentation that will require others to honor your directives. Just remember, nobody gets to pick the day that you have a medical emergency, or unfortunately die.

In principle, what you need to plan for is the same across the nation, but the legal requirements on a state by state basis are going to vary. Some states are marital property states providing specific spousal rights and other states recognize the individual. You will have to do some homework to find out what the requirements are in the location you live. I hope that you can find out what you generally need to know on your own, and use public and private sector resources to help. I will lay out what you need to consider in general terms. You will probably need the help of an expert in legally drafting and recording some of the documents. Remember you are protecting what is **rightfully yours** and requiring others to legally follow your directives.

Fortunately or unfortunately, there will be other people that will benefit from your death. I guess that is why these people are referred to as 'beneficiaries'. The financial structure in this country generally takes care of this when you open various kinds of accounts at banks and other financial institutions. Similar action takes place with insurance policies. After name, address, and other details related to you specifically as the account owner(s), the last page of the application form just above where you sign and date has a section for the naming of a beneficiaries. In the case of an individual account you are the single owner and get to name a primary and secondary beneficiary for the account. Upon your death and after all obligations to the account have been paid and/or your estate settled, the primary beneficiary will get the remaining balance. In the case of death of the primary beneficiary, the secondary beneficiary will get the account balance. For a joint account with two or more owners, the transfer of the balance to a beneficiary (primary or secondary) will take place after the death of the last named owner.

You can make changes to beneficiary as your needs require. Someone may no longer fit your requirements as a named beneficiary, passed away or for some other reason not currently qualify. A joint account will require agreement of all owners to make the change. This is something that you should review on an annual basis. Account owners should contact the issuing financial institution to make the changes. There are different requirements for retirement accounts than taxable accounts. I was not specific in recommendations of how you select the one to get your money and other resources when you are gone and can't do anything about it, but generally it will be next of kin (spouse, siblings, children, cousins, etc.), or in the case of no next of kin, friends or even charities.

So somewhere in your life you got married or were involved in a relationship that generated one or more children and the responsibilities that come with supporting dependents. You may also be providing care for others that require your help and qualify as dependents. So following on the theme you can't pick the day that you will be incapacitated or die, and no longer be able to care or support others, there is something very important you need to document. Naming of a guardian for your dependents becomes a directive for others to honor. If you don't document instructions or give a directive for guardianship of your dependents, some other decision maker could make an undesirable move that you can't control. The other decision maker is usually a government agency at the county or state level. So if you don't want your dependent parent or grandparent in a poorly managed care facility or you children in foster care, take the time to name a guardian.

This can be a difficult task to complete because you have to get cooperation and agreement from the party that will provide the care for the dependent. In many cases this requires out of pocket expenses on their part. But in most situations, the placement of the dependent will be with a family member or close acquaintance.

Remember that it is possible for you to designate money from your financial resources to support the dependent. So if a child goes to an aunt for guardianship, naming the aunt as a beneficiary would be reasonable. These advance directives are tied together. The next section of this chapter shows additional levels of estate planning to make it easier for next of kin to follow your directives.

A health care power of attorney, often referred to by some as a living will or health care directive, is important for individuals approaching the end of life on this planet. This document allows you to make decisions about how you want to be treated by medical professionals after you can no longer make decisions. Some people choose to have everything possible done to extend their lives and others want to be kept comfortable and die at home if possible without intervention. If you don't document your preferences, somebody else will be doing what *they think* you would want done or just do what they want done. In any case, since you aren't capable, you aren't part of the decisions and directives. So if you care about end of life planning, the health care directive is an important document.

Typically, you get to make decisions about your health care until you are determined to no longer have the capacity to make the decisions as determined after examination and written confirmation by medical professionals. That statement would be attached to the directive document and an agency agreement would be in effect allowing the primary designee to make health care decisions on your behalf. If the primary agent is unable or unwilling to make the decisions the documentation usually designates a secondary agent. Obviously while still capable, you need to discuss with the primary and secondary agents your desires on how health care is delivered.

Some treatments that can be included in the documentation relate to limitations of mental health treatment, admission to a nursing home or community based residential facility, provision for a feeding tube, DNR (Do Not Resuscitate) and a host of other specific treatments. Other items covered relate to organ donation, anatomical gifts and designation of the corpse for study.

Prior to the development of community hospitals, people died at home with care that was available for the time and area. If admitted to a hospital, typically the medical professionals will go to extraordinary measures to sustain life and prolong what is going to happen eventually. Health care directives and the advent of hospice care provide comfort and dignity to those facing terminal illnesses or wish to pass away without intervention.

Again the legal requirements will vary by state and need to be researched. Typically you will be able to find generic documentation from websites to use as a model to get an idea of the structure. Signature of principal (which is you); witnesses, registration and dissemination of copies are all part of the process. The health care directive is a document that needs periodic review and updating.

The next document you need when decision making capability is declining is the durable power of attorney. When the medical professionals determine you can no longer make decisions for yourself regarding health care, it is obvious that you can't make decisions relating to business and the expense of assets to pay the operating costs of a home and other bills relating to independent living. So here is where the second agency agreement becomes a necessity. This is a money decision, as you will be giving someone you trust the right to access your accounts to manage your financial life when you don't have the ability. Again terms and conditions will be in general terms due to state by state requirements and the limits of various levels of powers of attorney.

I mentioned the word 'durable' earlier, as this allows the power of attorney to have extended duration and broader application to your affairs. There are other types of powers of attorney that specify agency agreements and you can research these if you feel the need. The POA (Power of Attorney) will designate a primary agent to act in your behalf. If the primary agent is unable to serve then a secondary agent is named. Obviously these individuals should be aware of the arrangements when you establish the POA and be ready to serve your needs when the time comes.

The durable POA will typically allow the person to act as your agent to do many things legally relating the financial part of your life. These actions include but are not limited to: collect mail, handle financial transactions, legal actions, real estate dealings, safe deposit box access, exercise benefit rights, address tax return requirements, and a host of others. The agent should have the right to hire professionals to render necessary services, and the agent can collect reasonable compensation for labor and expenses. You need to set up an agent to do the work on your behalf, otherwise you don't know who will do it or if it will get done at all. This is another important step in managing your money.

You can no longer manage or even think about your money when you are dead. Unfortunate as it is, this is something we all have to experience. The next part of documentation is the will. The will is a wrap up or last testament to your life. They can be simple or complicated. It depends on the individual's situation regarding assets, next of kin, specific directives and a long list of other concerns. In the simplest terms a will needs to define who gets your property, who gets guardianship of minor children, who will manage property given to minor children, and who is named executor to carry out the directives of the will. As I said they can be complicated and you can research that on your own.

Your property goes to who you say you want to have it. However, with married couples, if you are the first to die, your personal property and assets typically go directly into the control of the surviving spouse. Assets owned jointly with you (whether it's your spouse or someone else), are automatically retained by the living owners. It's not uncommon for many people to be on their second or third marriage. You may not want your current (third) husband to get your pewter collection. There may be specific personal items that you want designated to go to others, and individually owned accounts to go to specific beneficiaries. Certain assets, inheritance and possessions obtained before the first, second (third or fourth) marriage are not always legal marital property. Each of you will need to have directives that clearly state who gets what. As awkward or uncomfortable as it may be, your directives need to be put in writing or the surviving spouse could automatically receive them, except on insurance policies or accounts where you've already formally named a beneficiary. However, if that beneficiary has passed then the account or asset could go to the current surviving spouse. You will then need to have copies of your directives and/or will held in confidence and legally filed by an attorney after death. Again annual review and updating as required is critically important.

We talked about guardianship in detail earlier in this segment and the thought that needs to go into taking care of minor children and dependents. The will is a document that can legally name the guardian and agent to care for the assets left to the minor children.

The will designates an executor or an individual to make sure that the terms of the will are carried out. The executor can be a relative, friend, or an independent third party. In the planning of these documents, the executor should be aware of your wishes and be able to assume and accomplish the responsibilities that come with being named executor.

Planning for death is not an easy task and the earlier in your life you start the exercise the better you will feel about doing it and you will get it done right if you follow the rules relating to periodic review and updating. Not everybody is going to be happy with the decisions you made, but they will get past their own selfish desires over time. Remember life is for **you** to live, and your death is an opportunity for you to reward the ones you loved and the ones that loved you.

Final Details Worksheet:

Have you done an inventory of your bills, debts, assets and personal belongings?_____

Have you taken the time to think about who you would like to have some or all of your belongings if you were to suddenly pass away?_____

Do you have enough life insurance to pay off your bills, debts and all costs related to your final interment?_____

If you have a spouse, children or dependants, do you have enough life insurance to provide for their financial security after all bills and debts are paid?_____

Do you have a will or detailed directives written out?_____

Do you have an executor named?_____

Do you update your will/directives once a year? On what date will you do this every year?_____

Do you review your assets and possessions annually? Do you make the necessary corrections regarding the names of people who are no longer in your life or added those who have recently entered your life?_____

Have you looked at your health insurance plan? Do you have enough, too little or more coverage than you (or your family) need?_____

Are you spending more money than necessary on insurances that you don't really need or that wouldn't benefit any of the people you love?_____

What types and levels of insurance coverage would give you peace of mind?_____

Closing summary:

Money is a renewable resource because you can always earn more of it. But it is also a finite and depleting resource. At any given moment you will only have a certain amount of it and if you don't keep an eye on it and hold it securely it will dwindle away.

Everything is an exchange. We exchange our time, labor and talent for cute little tokens called money. We then exchange that money for something else. We devote the vast portion of our life working to earn money so we can acquire "things." Most of those things are purely for our existence but many of those things make our life fun and exciting. Quite a few of those things allow for wonderful life experiences and others are a waste of our tokens.

As we mature in physical age, many of our acquisitions are no longer used by us or we have no need for them so we begin divesting and shedding some of those things. This is the natural cycle of a human life—acquiring things, using the things you acquire and then divesting yourself of them or passing them on to someone who will use them.

Things that bring you joy and great experiences are worthy of spending your money on. A ski boat is a fantastic toy while in your 20's and 30's. At age 50 it may become more of a burden than a pleasure. However, if you have children and grandchildren you may get joy out of watching them use it. I don't feel that *things* are a waste of money as long as you can afford them and they bring you genuine joy.

Be wary of the philosophy, "Just think about it and it will come your way." That's a nice start, but just thinking about something won't make it happen. I agree that the act of consciously thinking about and filling your mind with positive thoughts can work for intangibles such as emotions and feelings—feelings of contentment, happiness, joy and love. But just putting a picture of a Ferrari on your refrigerator won't put one in your garage. That picture can serve as a constant mental reminder of what you want, but getting one requires a rational thought process, it needs to be looked at in concrete form. Questions must be asked of yourself: HOW will I make it happen? What do I have to do (action/behavior) to earn enough money? Is it worth the exchange? Is it probable? Is it feasible?

This can be a painful thought process, because as you look at the facts, you might discover your own limitations and find that what you want isn't feasible or you realize how much work will be required and you perceive it as an insurmountable hurdle and become deflated. But that's when the fun of "doing" begins. That's when you ask yourself: What other goal might be just as good but have a higher probability? Who do I know that has done this? How did they do it? What are my strengths? What are my weaknesses? Am I willing to make the exchange of my time for money? Where's my pad of paper so I can start writing out a plan?

You may not get what you want, you may not even get what you need, but you'll certainly get what you get. Do what you can to make the best out of what you get. Balancing the truth of current conditions while pursuing goals is what will make for a happy existence.

I have been poor, broke, wealthy and varied gradations in between—traveling back and forth in the middle of them all during my life. Without hesitation I can say that living broke sucks. Realistic financial security and a sense of calm are my goals. I am not afraid of money but I must be ever vigilant to watch that I don't fall prey to its lustful pursuit. I cannot allow myself to feel as if I deserve money, but I will not apologize for earning it and living well.

My hope is that you feel you received something in return for your exchange of money for this book. I hope this book helps you find your own psychological comfort with money. I hope you become less fearful of money and think up your own creative ways to get the most utility and joyful experiences out of your money.

Make your money work for you and get the most out of every penny you earn, spend and invest. Make every exchange count.

Money is worthless until something is done with it—so do things with it that will bring you and your loved ones a comfortable, secure and pleasant existence. Money may not buy you everything, but it can buy you a lot of things. Money may not bring you happiness, but living broke sure does suck.

Mark A. Tuschel

Afterword

The man who wrote the Foreword, a segment in chapter 12 and contributed to this Afterword is a friend of mine. His name is **Jeff Rendall**. I am under the belief that he is a wealthy man, yet he is considerate, helpful towards others and never showy. I respect and admire him. I have no idea of his net worth or wealth—it doesn't matter and it's none of my business. I was drawn to him because of his behaviors towards people and his words. I made him my mentor without his knowledge or his permission. (Making people my secret mentor puts less pressure on them.)

Jeff and I are very similar yet vastly different. We hold many of the same values:

- A dollar is a dollar.
- Never apologize for living well.
- Never apologize for earning money through honest ways.
- Spend less than you earn by having a budget. (Jeff calls it a 'plan'.)
- Tracking your expenses, designating your income to specific areas and creating a budget DOES NOT require an accounting degree. It is basic math.
- The time spent (as boring and mentally taxing as it may be), collecting, analyzing and planning your own personal financial data is well worth it.
- Don't rob yourself of pleasantries because you're trying to amass wealth—enjoy a little now but continue to save for the future.
- Continuously learn and expand your knowledge. Make yourself valuable to the marketplace and the world.

- Always think how you can get the most utility out of your resources of money, time, talent, mind and physical abilities.
- Money isn't everything—it's the ONLY thing.

But here's how we are different: Jeff buys brand new cars, I only buy used or dealer demos. I don't think I'll ever buy a brand new car. I don't think Jeff is wrong or foolish with his car purchases. I happen to know that he keeps his cars for 10 to 20 years. He gets a lot of utility out of them. He keeps them well maintained. When it's time for a different car he never trades his in. He either sells this "cream puff" privately or gives it to a friend or relative in need of a reliable car.

I could also say that Jeff is a much more conservative saver and investor than I am, but that's not completely true. Jeff observed that I buy a lot of volatile and risky stocks that "he wouldn't even look at." I agree that I do, but I am conservative in my desire for returns. I'll take a .06 cent return on 10,000 shares. $600 profit is REAL money to me, especially if that happens within a few hours of purchasing the stock. An uneducated investor might say, "But it could keep going higher!" It could, but it could also crater. A $600 profit is REAL money to me. Plus I have all of my capitol back and can invest that—along with my profits—into another stock that will hopefully move up .05 cents.

Neither Jeff or I are deluded by percentages, we look at REAL earnings and REAL money. I must give Jeff credit for taking the time to explain this to me. "Don't be deluded by percentages. Look at REAL money." He illuminated me. I readjusted my investing strategy and stay flexible so I can readjust as needed.

Investing isn't a contest and percentages can be misleading. When someone brags to me, "I have an 18% return on my investments for the year," I ask, "That's great, but how much did you earn? Is that 18% return in cash or value? Because you can't buy food with value, only with cash."

Which would you rather have?: 18% *value* increase on a $10,000 investment? OR a measly .75% cash return on $1,000,000?

Here's the math: 18% of $10,000 = $1,800 but .75% of $1,000,000 = **$7,500**.

"Sounds great Mark but I don't have a million dollars you jerk." Well, neither did I. But as long as I kept churning my $10,000 into investments, getting a .05 to .10 cent increase, selling and buying another stock, getting another .05 cent increase, selling, etc. by the end of the year I spent and reinvested a little over $1,000,000. Leaving me with a yearend **cash** balance in excess of $17,500 (which is a **75%** return on my original cash) but less than 1% return on each investment.

Allow me to address your questions and objections. I grant you that my example is simplified and would work in a perfect situation. All situations aren't perfect. Some of those stock positions returned less than .05 cents per share but a few were in excess of .25 cents per share.

You might say, "You spent a ton of money on brokerage fees. How much did the brokerage make off of you?" Who cares? In fact, I hope they made money. Share the wealth. Their trading platform allowed me the opportunity to earn $7,500 that I put in my own pocket.

"You have to pay taxes on your gains." So what? I'm proud to pay taxes. Paying taxes means that I earned a profit and I have REAL money now—which I can reinvest and keep reinvesting— not just value or *unrealized worth*. If you're smart enough to earn money you should be smart enough (or educate yourself) to use every legal tax deduction allowable. If I've already paid taxes on profits I can't be taxed on them again in the future. I have what is rightly mine and the government has been paid their piece of the action. Render unto Caesar what is Caesar's—but not a penny more.

My way of investing is **NOT** right for everyone. I do this as a fulltime job—investing and trading IS my job. As my portfolio worth has grown I have purchased some stocks and bonds that I will hold for a long time (but I will occasionally leverage against them—I want my money to work for ME and not just sit there).

As I mentioned in the chapter on investing, I believe that most people should take advantage of every investment tool their employer offers and should also make some investments of their own. Index Funds, sector specific Mutual Funds, individual stocks, Money Market accounts, Government Bonds and Certificate of Deposit.

You want to live broke? That's your choice. You want to burn through every penny you have, with your spending limited only by how much you can earn? That's your choice. Anyone can live broke, it doesn't take much skill. Living well and wealthy requires thinking, self-control and time. I'm confident that you have the ability to nurture those properties. Don't rob yourself of a comfortable existence.

By: Jeff Rendall

Before you started reading this book you probably felt incompetent, and uncomfortable in the way you managed money and the catchy title of this book stimulated you to purchase a copy and start to generate success in your financial life. Hopefully it provides guidance you will use multiple times to gain new skills and get insight to improve life for you and those around you.

As stated in the foreword, and many times through the book, **Money is the only thing.** The world we live in is a complicated system where currency is required to exchange for products and services. The development and application of electronics and digital memory have allowed this system to perform instantaneously and require everyone to function electronically in financial transactions. This requires the use of recognized banks with functional accounts and attached credit and debit cards.

Hopefully you have gained confidence from absorbing key strategies from this book and moved forward in your quest to utilize your income in a way that avoids the pitfalls and traps that reduce the buying power of you money. Successful relationships with financial institutions and development and utilization of both short and long term credit should be a reality for you.

To move out of poverty and leave being broke behind requires forming strategies for the evolutionary steps needed to be successful. Forming your strategies should not be a long and time consuming process. But as you finish the first operational cycle of a specific strategy, you will find that the circumstances will have changed somewhere and require you to reapply some thought on how to get to the end goal you established. This will get you to apply your thinking in a continuous improvement loop. You will plan your action, deploy it, check results of your action, and re-plan how you will do it better the next time. You need to remember that this **plan, act, check and react process** will provide increased success in everything you do as part of your life.

Successful management of money and everything else you do in your life requires passion. It is important to believe in yourself and have the conviction to be successful in everything you need to complete. You need to take this energy and use it to influence others around you to understand that your decisions are the right ones and based on research, measurement and fact. That means you will be doing your own research and learning from the experience of others to get the skills to continuously improve your money management. The hardest part will be to stay focused and execute your plan. Every decision will have some risk associated with it because money is on the line to be saved, lost or used in a way that boosts the value produced in a purchase or the yield generated in an investment.

Financial success will eventually put you in a position of recognized leadership for you and/or your immediate family. Over time your influence will grow as others see or experience you climbing out of the downward spiral of poverty and being broke.

This will require integrity and being honest and forthcoming with yourself and others. The lack of excuses, and dealing with fact, will strengthen your bonds with family, friends, and those that you are engaged with in financial relationships. Some will dislike your decisions, but you need to do what's right for you and key to success of your financial plan. This is part of 'tough love'.

As your skills develop, your self-confidence will grow and this will open you to accept ideas and information from other individuals and sources that increase your knowledge. As knowledge and self-confidence grow, you will need to stretch your goals. If you saved an amount or percentage in a specific budget item with your new measurement skills, find a way to increase the saved amount in the next cycle and keep doing this until there is no more savings to squeeze out.

Don't forget to reward yourself and members of your team if you have one. Unrecognized successes will eventually turn you stale to the continuous process of taking cost out and adding value to your lifestyle. A periodic celebration is needed to stimulate you to step back and reenergize your efforts. The only thing that matters is effective management of monetary income and expense to provide the opportunity to live a full and enjoyable life and share it with others.

After Thought as a Contributor to the Book

As a casual friend of Mark's I offered to write the foreword and afterword to this book and some content to the body of the book through the writing process. My upbringing, educational background and life experiences are far different than Mark's, but we share a common goal: Helping others help themselves.

My financial knowledge is self taught over decades through reading books, periodicals, dealing with professionals in investment and brokerages and recently the mountains of knowledge on the internet. There is no easy way to gain all this knowledge. It is a full time job. Fortunately for me, my educational background and work experience was focused on utilization of math and science skills, logic, problem solving, risk assessment and process and project management where positive financial performance was required. I can assure you this was a significant advantage in managing money and investing. Your skill set development is up to you. If you don't stay focused on, plan, act, measure and react every day, financial success will not happen.

I need to switch from first person in writing this because my success was really our success. My spouse and her skills work ethic were also a big part of our financial success and investment plans. We started buying investments in our early thirties shortly after getting married. It became a two income household and combining living expenses provided money or capital that could be invested. We had no debt other than a mortgage on our primary residence and an occasional auto purchase. Strategically we were looking to make the transition in twenty to twenty-five years from working for others for their money to working for ourselves and letting our investments work for us. We had the ability to annually maximize contributions to IRA's, pension and other defined benefit retirement programs that were tax deferred and had compounded future value. These plans are resources that are available through employers and the tax codes and everyone needs find a level where they can take advantage of them. We also were able to generate significant value in taxable accounts. All of these accounts were diversified in stocks, bonds, insurance and other financial instruments.

There have been three times where we were 'blown up' by financial market down turns and lost up to fifty percent of our invested wealth. We knew the balance of risk and reward. We were required to work harder and smarter to make up for the losses. At the same time we continued to work professionally to meet everyday needs and maintain the contributions to accounts for future needs. In some cases it took more than six years of compounding gains to get back to the level before the downturn event. Some event will generate a loss of assets or a huge increase in spending in your life. This will happen to you and is just a part of the journey.

There is no one right way to financial success and the ability to live comfortably, not worrying about income and expense. It takes a lot of knowledge both from this book and other sources and hard work to make it happen. Even when you are living life without worrying about where you will get the money to pay the next bill, you will still be planning how to get the most value for the lowest cost, because you have developed the mind set and skills to manage one of the most important things in life – Money

Acknowledgements

"If I spend all my time with myself, the only opinions I would ever hear would be my own."

There are so many people in my life that must be acknowledged for their help. There are those who have spent their time and talents reviewing and editing this work. Not only are they skilled editors, they are friends. I would like to give them public recognition: Dana Meredith, Jeff Rendall. There are also all of the people who spent their time allowing me to interview them and discussing this project.

So many people have engaged me in spirited conversations, debating with me about religion, politics, financial markets, capitalism, money, education, human behavior, you name it. They help me question my premises. Not question my beliefs and principles, but to check my data. By questioning my premises I am required to study more and ultimately gain more knowledge. You challenge my mind.

I acknowledge my friends and family who stand by me and care about me. I appreciate it when they say, "Stop working for a few minutes and enjoy what you have earned." When they say "earned," they're not just referring to money, but to the joys of friendship, relaxation and experiences.

Additionally, any mathematical errors, misspellings, errors in punctuation, poor grammar, run-on sentences and stupid statements are completely my own. I had final authorization of everything in this book.

Finally, as arrogant as this may sound, I wish to acknowledge myself. Without self-discipline, effort and conscious planning, this book never would have been completed. I would still be drunk and broke today. I am proud of myself.

I sincerely wish that your life turns out better than you ever imagined,

Mark A. Tuschel

About the writer:

Mark A. Tuschel.

I prefer to consider myself a "writer" and not an author. Author sounds too snooty. I'm unimpressed with myself. As a writer I pass my thoughts along to those who are interested in reading them. Writing requires me to clearly define what is in my mind, put it on paper (or a screen), and convey those thoughts and meanings into another person's mind. I like that challenge.

I am an Unapologetic Capitalist. I hold no allegiance to any political party. I support whoever has a good idea.

I openly admit that I am cheap. People who know me say, "Oh Mark, you're just frugal." No I'm not, I'm cheap. I don't cheap out on quality, I mostly buy quality products. I don't cheap out with my friends—I share what I have and what I can afford.

I am cheap with myself and with my money. I'm not greedy or money grubbing, but I'm cheap in that I won't buy something simply because I can afford it or it falls within my budget. I follow my own advice and wait before making large purchases (unless it's an emergency). I'm cheap because I think through my purchases. "Do I really need this? Do I already own something that will suffice? Will this enhance my life? Will this bring an experience of joy?" I live within a budget and I always pay myself first. If I changed my behavior and became looser with my money I would slowly begin eroding at my own financial security. I've seen me do it in the past. I know from experience that living broke sucks.

My personal goal is to continue honing my craft as a writer. The more people I meet, the more I learn. With that, I hope to expand my personal creativity. I write for my own enjoyment, full gratification comes when other people also enjoy my work. I'm not fond of criticism, but I do welcome your feedback. Thank you for spending your valuable time reading something I have created.